The Collector's Guide to

MASKS

The Collector's Guide to
MASKS

TIMOTHY TEUTEN

BRACKEN BOOKS

The Collector's Guide to Masks

This edition first published in 1995 by Bracken Books,
an imprint of Random House UK Ltd,
Random House, 20 Vauxhall Bridge Road,
London SW1V 2SA

Reprinted 1996

The chapter on European Masks was written by Mike Hitchcock at the
University of Hull.

ISBN 1 85891 201 6

Printed and bound in Singapore

PUBLISHER'S NOTE

Prices for masks sold at specific auctions are given in the local
currency with the date of sale; where there is more than one
mask in a single image the reader should read the dimensions
and prices from left to right. All other prices mentioned are given
in £ sterling followed by US$ in brackets; the exchange rate has
been calculated at £1 to US$1.65.

CONTENTS

INTRODUCTION

Masks as a serious subject for the collector are a relatively recent phenomenon. It is only in the past thirty years that auction houses have begun to devote sales exclusively to tribal art. Prior to that, collecting masks and tribal art was the preserve of relatively few collectors, who were doubtless regarded as eccentric by their contemporaries, and who were consequently able to buy masks and other tribal artefacts for sums that seem extraordinary today.

Even many museums failed to appreciate the importance of their collections and before the Second World War were happy to exchange their masks and other artefacts for pieces of local farm machinery and the like considered far more worthy of preservation. In the 1930s, for instance, James Hooper went to the West Country to visit a museum that was disposing of its surplus stock and noticed a girl wearing a pair of sealskin boots washing down a car. When he enquired where she had obtained them, he was told that they had been rescued from a cartload of similar items sent to the local incinerator the previous day. Many such horror stories have been recorded. The catalogues of dealers in 'ethnographical specimens' such as Oldman and Webster in the early years of this century make very interesting reading. The prices of masks and figures are similar to those of clubs and other weapons, the aesthetic quality of a piece having little bearing on the price and all such items being regarded as 'curios' rather than works of art.

Today most of the early collections brought back from European colonies have been dispersed and the supply of fine, early specimens is therefore very limited. Prices are consequently high, and masks can sell at auction today for in excess of £200,000 (US $330,000). In fact, in 1989 the world record price for a piece of African art topped the million-pound mark. Many of the masking traditions described in this book, however, are still alive today and are a vital component of the society in which they are still found. In some areas, where the tradition has died or been weakened, masquerading has been or is being revived. Tourism, too, has played its part: in Bali, for instance, increasing numbers of visitors have enjoyed the per-

Olmec, Mexico, wood
*Masks in this style (**above left**) but carved from stone date back to the origins of the masquerading tradition in Central America. Sometimes the mask was embellished with semi-precious stones.*

Kwele, Gabon, wood
*This striking, stylized mask (**right**) represents an antelope. There is a wide range of masks carved by the various tribes of equatorial Africa; more information about such masks starts on page 32.*

formances of the *wayang topeng*, and in Africa since the 1940's some masquerades have been choreographed so that they may be performed in hotels. However, there is an increasing awareness of the need for preserving traditions throughout the world, and this has led to further, more serious revivals, as is the case in Vanuatu, where customs are seen as essential to the health and well-being of the community. For the new collector there is therefore a steady supply of new masks coming onto the market, not all

of which are made exclusively to satisfy the demand of tourists and dealers, and many of these can be obtained by collectors at modest prices.

The wooden face mask springs to most people's minds when the word mask is used, but in fact the variety of mask materials varies as much as the forms they take. Stone, gold, silver, bronze, hide, paper, cloth, palm spathe, woven or plaited fibre and lacquer are or have in the past been used. It must be remembered, however, that a mask is only a small, albeit important, part of the masquerader's costume, which would often consist of elaborate and colourful garments covering the wearer from head to foot. Divorced from its context it is often impossible to identify the character represented, or perhaps even the tribal group that made it.

Basically, a mask is a disguise. Its function may be to personify spirits, gods or ancestors, to assume social control, to educate or to elude responsibility for one's actions. The use of masks is almost exclusively restricted to men—even when, as is often the case, the characters represented are female. There are notable exceptions, however, such as the Sande society of Sierra Leone, in which the females wear the blackened helmet masks called *sowei*, the role of the male being relegated to the joker, or *gongoli*. Masking traditions are found in all continents with the notable exception of Australia, where the Aborigines have instead developed a system of body painting. The use of masks is generally restricted to forested areas, though again there are exceptions, notably the Inuit tradition (which may not date back beyond the first European contact).

Only a very small selection of the masking traditions from around the world can be mentioned in this book. But the illustrations will, I hope, indicate the variety that is to be found, and tempt you to investigate the subject further. A vast number of scholarly books exist on masks, and a selection of them is listed at the end of the book.

Alaska, wood
*This mask (**below**) would have been carved by a shaman to represent a spirit he had seen. The distorted features would inspire amazement in the spectators at the shaman's power to communicate with the spirit world.*
Height: 6¼in (16cm)

*Lower Sepik River New Guinea, wood (**right**)*
Height: 9½in (28cm)

Tolai, Gazelle peninsula, east New Britain, Papua New Guinea
These dukduk *masks (**left**) are up to 53⅜in (210cm) high.*

AFRICAN MASKS

African masks and headdresses reflect ceremonial traditions established many centuries ago. However, the perishable materials from which most of these masks are made mean that, despite the antiquity of many of the styles and cultures, only a few extant examples, such as bronze Benin masks, date from before the nineteenth century.

African masks first began to receive widespread attention from artists, critics and collectors in the early years of the twentieth century. At this time, a series of revolutionary art movements—Cubism, Fauvism and so on—overturned the conventions that had governed Western art since the Renaissance, and painters and sculptors such as Picasso, Braque and Epstein were enormously stimulated by the energy and freedom of 'primitive' art. These three great artists and several of their contemporaries had fine collections of African tribal art, including masks, and many examples of direct influence from the objects they owned have been traced in their work. Their love of African masks was genuine and deep, but it was also severely limited, for they responded to them purely as aesthetic objects and had little or no knowledge of their place in the cultures that produced them. To the makers and users of the masks, they are not simply beautiful ceremonial or ornamental objects, but rather an essential part of their spiritual lives. It is only when something is known of this context that the imaginative richness of African masks can be appreciated, and such knowledge can add greatly to the enjoyment that collectors derive from them.

Africa is an enormous continent and its size and diversity are reflected in the huge variety of masks made there. Nevertheless, in discussing masks, the continent can be divided into various broad areas. Two of these areas are by far the most important: west Africa; and the Zaire basin and equatorial Africa. In other areas, masking traditions have either ceased to exist or have never been of comparable importance. Africa north of the Sahara, for example, no longer has a living masking tradition and has tended to gravitate so strongly towards Mediterranean and Islamic culture that it is usually excluded from discussions of African traditional art.

Dogon, Mali, wood
*The rectangular forms of this mask (**above left**) are typical of the Dogon. The mask, called* walu, *represents an antelope and is one of the most popular Dogon masks.*

Bena-Biombo, Zaire, wood, raffia
*The bands of triangular decoration in reddish brown, black and white (**right**) are typical of the Bena-Biomba and neighbouring Pende.*
Height: 15in (38cm)

WEST AFRICA

Of the many groups in west Africa that have been well studied and documented, the one whose art is perhaps most popular with collectors is the Dogon of central Mali. The Dogon live on the Bandiagara escarpment, a long stretch of cliffs east of the River Niger. Dogon villages are an extraordinary sight, the simple mud-brick buildings with thatched roofs clinging like limpets to the stark rockface behind. The Dogon are farmers, their principal crop being millet, which they produce from a land of poor soil and low rainfall. Islam has penetrated to this region, but it has modified rather than eliminated the masking tradition, for example in encouraging the use of simple geometric designs, not only for masks but also for delineating farmland.

Religious ceremonies among the Dogon are principally concerned with the spirits of ancestors. All Dogon men become members of the masked dancing society—*Ava*—and perform at funerals and at the *Dama* rituals that take place several years after the funeral of an important man of the community (preparations require considerable time and money). Several hundred masks may be required, and large quantities of food and millet beer are distributed to add prestige to the deceased and his family. The masked dancers escort the soul of the deceased from the village and throw it into the bush.

Several types of masks are used on these occasions (more than 70 were listed in the 1930s). Those made of wood usually represent animals or birds and are generally of rectangular shape, with two square or oblong eyeholes, a form that is thought to reflect the appearance of the mosques of the area. Perhaps the most distinctive and familiar to collectors are the *kanaga* masks. These are surmounted by a superstructure consisting of a vertical bar crossed by two horizontal bars with vertical projections at each end. This has been said to represent God, and at the same time the upper bar may represent the sky and the lower one the earth. During the performance the masquerader bends down, bringing the top of the superstructure in contact with the ground. The masks are painted in white and black and are worn with a plaited fibre headcovering and an elaborate costume. It consists of a vest worn with cloth strips sewn with cowrie shells, a pair of indigo leg coverings over which the dancer wears skirts of red, yellow and black dyed fibres, and dyed fibre armbands. Several of these masks are danced together and there seems to be no objection if the dancers are witnessed by outside observers.

Rarer, but similar in style to the *kanaga* masks, are the *sim* masks. These have a similar superstructure, but of more fragile and slender form, which sways as the masquerader dances and is said to represent a human spirit. The mask that covers the face represents an antelope, with 'ears' at the sides and two deep grooved channels for the eyeholes. Mask and super-

structure are joined by a pierced lozenge and the whole is painted with chevrons (V-shapes) and zigzags. More commonly, antelope masks are found without this superstructure, but with horns and more naturalistic ears. Other animals represented in Dogon masks include monkeys, crocodiles and rhinoceroses.

Humans are also represented in the *Dama* ceremonies, although the masks representing them are usually of cloth, fibre and cowrie shells rather than wood. They may represent neighbouring tribes, such as the Bambara, Fulani and Tuareg, or sometimes Europeans and Arabs of particular groups from within their own community, such as blacksmiths and other craftsmen. The *samana* mask is a rare exception in that it is wooden and represents a foreign warrior.

Gurunsi, Burkina Faso, wood, early twentieth century
Many of the masks of Burkina Faso represent animals,
although it is often difficult to identify the species. This
*mask (**above**) appears to be an antelope.*
Height: 14in (35.5cm)   Christie's London 1989, £990

Bambara, Mali, wood
The horizontal form of the chi wara *headdress (**left**) is*
one of the most popular and widely available of West
African masks. The dancer wearing this male example
would have been accompanied by a female.

Although it has similar angular features to the animal masks, it is usually distinguished by three vertical striations on each cheek. The dancer holds a sword and lance and performs a mock battle with an invisible enemy. He also jokes rudely with the dancers wearing female masks (who don carved representations of breasts) and interacts with the audience.

An important ceremony, known as *Sigi,* is held once every 60 years to commemorate the mythical first death of an ancestor among the Dogon. A tall mask, sometimes measuring as much as 15ft (4.5m) in height, is carved in each community on this occasion and is said to represent a snake. These masks, called *imina na* or 'mother of masks', were not intended to be worn, but were carried or simply viewed in a stationary position. Some ancient examples survive in museums and private collections and may be as much as 200 years or more old.

To the south-west of the Dogon, the Bambara (also called Bamana) produce several types of mask associated with ancestors and funerals. However, they are best known among collectors of African art for what must be among the most familiar of all African carvings—the antelope headdresses called *chi wara.* These are danced in rituals associated with the planting and harvesting of millet. According to Bambara mythology; it was the water spirit Faro, in the form of an antelope, who first taught man to work the fields. The masks are danced in pairs, a male and a female, during the planting and harvest seasons to ensure crop fertility.

Although all masks should be seen when danced, this is particularly true of the *chi wara*, which make a marvellously stirring sight when moving across a skyline. The headdresses are attached to fibre caps from which fibre strands descend to cover the dancers' bodies, which are bent over for the entire performance, leaning on two short sticks. The male is more athletic in his movements and sometimes screeches, while the female, more gentle, remains silent.

There are three distinct styles of headdress. Tall, vertical examples are said to come from the area of Segu. The male is often represented with a large, curved neck and mane pierced with bands of triangles, with tall, almost vertical horns and a diminutive stylized body. The female also has tall vertical horns and a slender neck and can be clearly distinguished by the young antelope standing on her back. This is probably the type most frequently encountered today and large numbers are now made to supply the tourist trade in Bamako and elsewhere. The carvers are also becoming skilled at reproducing dark, glossy patinas and signs of wear that, under normal circumstances, are a sign of considerable age. Other *chi wara* can be divided into two main categories, low horizontal ones, which are said to come from Beledugu, and ones in which the antelope is highly stylized, from Oussulu.

Among the other mask types of the Bambara asociated with the male initiation societies is the *n'tomo*, which has a stylized humanoid face surmounted by a row of vertical projections inset with cowrie shells and red abrus seeds. The number of projections varies between four and ten and indicates the gender of the masks; three, six and nine indicate masculinity, four and eight femininity, and two, five and seven androgyny. The hyena mask, with a long, oval face, slender nose, pricked ears and pierced square eyes, is much sought after by collectors. Nearly all Bambara masks have a dark patina, which can be glossy or crusty with age and use.

Across the border from Mali, several mask-producing tribes are found in Burkina Faso. The principal groups of the area are the Kurumba, Mossi, Gurunsi, Bwa, Bobo, Lobi and Tusyan. The Lobi are famous for figurative sculpture, but do not have a masking tradition. The Mossi produce an enormous variety of masks, mostly representing totemic animals, spirits and occasionally humans, through which they commune with ancestors. They are usually made from the wood of the cotton tree, which is easy to carve and light to wear, although also prone to insect damage. Consequently, each year after the harvest but before the masquerade season commences (usually in February), the masks are taken from the village to a swamp or river and immersed with heavy stones for several weeks to kill any infestations. This removes all the pigment from the surface with the exception of black, which is not water soluble. The masks are then repainted by the young initiates; the thickness of the

black pigment can therefore help to indicate the age of a mask. Among the Mossi, some of the most frequently encountered totems are the hawk, ram, small antelope, large antelope, hornbill and human albino. The sizes vary enormously, from small crests worn on the top of the head or at an angle on the forehead to large masks covering the whole face. The degree of naturalism also varies; some totems are clearly identifiable, while others are abstracted, although there is usually one particular feature that stands out and helps with problems of identification.

A particularly distinct type of mask is found among the Mossi of Yatenga province. Known as *karanga*, it consists of a whitened oval face with a vertical, raised, notched ridge down the middle between the two triangular eyeholes. Above the face is a small antelope head with long horns and this is surmounted by a tall slender plank pierced with geometric shapes and carved and painted with geometric ornament. Another type of mask from the same area of Burkino Faso, known as *karanwemba*, has a similar face but is surmounted by a female figure.

The adjacent Gurunsi and Bwa use animal masks similar to those of the Mossi, and in addition they make a plank mask, with a circular face surmounted by a large rectangular plank. This has a crescent finial carved and painted with typical geometric ornament. The Bwa are also known for broad horizontal masks, more than 4ft (1.2m) in width, representing hawks, with hooked projections from the top of the head, and for even broader masks, sometimes more than 8ft (2.4m) in width, representing butterflies.

Despite the enormous variety of mask forms from the area, there is a unifying feature that distinguishes most of the masks from Burkina Faso—surface decoration. Most of them are extensively carved and painted with geometric ornament (bands of triangles, zigzags and lozenges, for example) in white, black and reddish brown. Usually traditional pigments are used, but recently commercially produced paints have been available, and this has broadened the range of colours. Such splendid painted decoration is a characteristic feature of a type of headdress carved by the Kurumba, who live to the north of the Mossi. It represents an antelope, the totemic emblem of most of the Kurumba clans. These headdresses are relatively naturalistic in form, having a long neck and slender head with tall horns above. The surface is painted with a vibrant pattern of zigzags and spots. Although many fine old specimens have found their way into museums and private collections, the majority available to the collector today are made expressly for the art market.

The tribes living in the forested areas along the Guinea Coast, from Guinea-Bissau in the west to Cameroon in the east, are among the most prolific in Africa for wood carving and for mask production. In the far west, off the coast of Guinea-Bissau, are the Bissagos Islands, home of the Bijugo, who produce a

Ekoi, Nigeria, wood, skin, rattan, early twentieth century
The large spiralling horns of this headdress (**left**) represent the ceremonial coiffure worn by Ekoi women. Although very varied in their forms, Ekoi masks are distinguished by the covering of antelope skin that is frequently used.

Nafana, Ivory Coast or Ghana, wood
This style of large mask (**above**) would seem to derive from an early type of which only two examples are known to exist. The style disappeared, and re-emerged in about 1915. Many examples appeared on the market around 1950, apparently made for expatriates.
Height: 51³/₁₆in (130cm)

Bijugo, Bissagos Islands, wood, horns, fibre, twentieth century
Bovine masks, the most familiar of a number of naturalistic masks representing animals, were danced by members of age-grade societies. Other masks represented sharks and sawfish.

variety of masks principally for use in 'age-grade' initiation ceremonies. The masks are carved by trained artists, sometimes in large numbers, and are then stored in granaries in preparation for use in the major festivals. First-grade initiates, aged between 12 and 17, wear small headdresses representing fish or domesticated animals, while older grades wear larger headdresses representing more dangerous animals. These include sharks and rays, but most familiar are the bull helmet masks. They cover the entire head of a dancer and are carved and painted in a naturalistic style, with real horns and often with green bottle-glass

eyes. They sometimes also have dilated nostrils and a protruding tongue. During the masquerade, the dancer scrapes the ground with his foot and charges at the crowd. Although physically mature, an adult is not considered socially responsible until he has passed through the age grades, after which he abandons his mask and no longer takes part in masquerades.

One of the most massive of all types of African masks is found among the Baga, who live along the coast of neighbouring Guinea. These are the masks popularly known as *nimba*, although more correctly called *damba*. *Damba* is not a sacred spirit, but rather

Dan, Ivory Coast, wood,
twentieth century
Female masks,
representing the ideal of
Dan beauty, are among the
most popular of west
African masks. This small
example was formerly in
the collection of Mrs
Webster Plass.
Height: 6⅞in (17.3cm)

represents the idea of women who have borne children. Their veneration is considered essential to ensure both human and crop fertility. The mask consists of a large bust, with cantilevered head on four pronged supports. Two holes for the eyes are carved between the breasts, and a long fibre fringe covers the dancer's body. Early masks of this type are rare and they have not been danced in Guinea since the 1950s, when the last 'genuine' examples were exported by the French. Large examples have, in recent years, appeared on the market although the artists who made them have often, apparently, been unable to resist the temptation of exaggerating the features. On several occasions I have attempted to 'test' the authenticity of such heavy masks by lying the mask on the ground and trying to crawl inside on my back between the prongs to see if it is possible for a dancer to put his head inside and see through the eyeholes. This has made me aware of the immense weight of the masks and has made me appreciate the considerable strength that was required to support them in a masquerade. Smaller masks worn in a similar manner to the *damba* are known as *damba-pa-fet*. These are carved as a small head above a stylized plank-like torso, with the breasts in relief.

17

Mama, northern Nigeria, wood, twentieth century
Masks from northern Nigeria rarely appear on the
market. This stylized buffalo mask (above) is one of the
more familiar types.
Height: 17³/₄in (45 cm)

Mende, Sierra Leone, wood, fibre, twentieth century
These masks (left), danced by the women's secret society
among the Mende and neighbouring tribes, are still made
and used today.
Height: 46¹/₂in (118 cm)

Closely related to the Baga are the Nalu, a much smaller tribe to the north and west. They make a type of large mask known as *banda*, which is worn horizontally on the head. Measuring 5ft (1.5m) or more in length, it combines features both of humans and of several types of animal, having long jaws with carved teeth, a slender nose, long ears and intertwined snake-like elements at the top of the head. The entire surface is carved in low relief, often with florets and motifs reflecting Portuguese influence, and is painted in various colours including unusual pinks, greens and mauves.

The only masking tradition in Africa reserved exclusively for women is found among the tribes spanning the border of Sierra Leone and Liberia, such as the Mende, Temne and Sherbro. Here the women have a secret society called *Sande*, counterpart to the men's society, *Poro*. Both these societies are concerned with the initiation of youths, boys and girls being confined to separate camps. Boys are taught agricultural skills and crafts such as basketry and the making of nets and traps, as well as learning how to play the drum and sing the songs of the *Poro* society. The skills taught to the girls include homecrafts, childcare, sexual matters, singing and dancing. In this they are assisted by masked spiritual helpers who also escort the initiates to and from the camp. The masked spirits do not speak, but communicate in a graceful language of gesture and dance. At the end of this period (which traditionally lasts about three years) the girls emerge as women ready for marriage.

The helmet masks worn by these spirit helpers are called *sowei* and are said to represent the ideal of Mende beauty. The facial features are small, with a high forehead and usually an elaborate coiffure, sometimes surmounted by an animal or bird. The rings about the neck denote the plumpness of a wealthy women—a sign of beauty and affluence among these tribes. The blackened surface is rubbed with palm oil to achieve a dark glossy patina. Although worn by women, these masks are carved by men. They are still made and used today, and a large number appear on the market. It is sometimes difficult to differentiate between those made for tribal use and those made for tourists, but the ones that are too small to be worn comfortably must have been made for the art market. *Sowei* move slowly and gracefully and, to lighten the atmosphere created by these stately females, a joker called *gongoli* is introduced. Formerly he wore a large rough mask with domed forehead, long nose and projecting ears, but old re-used *sowei* are often danced today.

There are several mask-producing tribes in the Ivory Coast, among them the Dan, whose masks are highly prized among collectors of African tribal art. The majority of Dan masks represent spirits who are believed to dwell in the mountains. In fact, 'represent' is not really the right word to use in this context, since for the Dan the mask *is* the spirit and it is said that when a mask is lying on the ground one can sometimes hear it 'grinding its teeth'. When a mask is damaged and no longer usable it must not simply be discarded, but must be treated with respect. The capturing of masks was one of the prime aims of war campaigns, although a new owner could not immediately wear a captured mask—he had to wait until the mask spirit acknowledged him. Sometimes several generations might pass before the mask accepted its new ownership. The masked spirits speak in a language unintelligible to the audience; it has to be translated for them by means of an interpreter.

The Dan today recognize 11 different categories of mask, but identification for the collector is often by no means easy. For the spectator at a masquerade this would be made clear, partly by the actions of the dancer, but also by the type of headdress attached to the mask. There were various types of cloth headdress and others of feathers and leaves, which are usually absent in specimens in collections and museums. Most Dan masks are approximately life-size and all are worn vertically over the face of the masquerader. They are either male or female; masks with oval faces, narrow eyes and fairly naturalistically carved mouths and noses are usually female and represent the Dan ideal of female beauty, while male masks are more varied and include all the types of animal mask.

Of the 11 categories, some are easily identifiable. The masks of the bird masquerade, *Gegon* (the most popular masquerade among the northern Dan), usually have slender eyes surrounded by applied metal bands, and a long beak-like nose with articulated lower jaw with attached fur from the colobus monkey. Masks of the hooked-stick masquerade, in which the dancer beats spectators with a hooked stick, are of animal form, often representing a cow, bird or monkey. The eyes are either deep-set triangular apertures or cylindrical projections, and cheeks are usually conceived as bulging pyramids. The masks have large projecting mouths and beaks, occasionally with large teeth. Masks used in the war masquerade, *Bugle,* are roughly carved, with bulging cylindrical eyes and a large mouth inset with large teeth. They are often covered in a crusty patina resulting from the application of sacrificial blood and chewed kola nuts.

The fire-prevention masquerade was at one time widespread among the northern Dan, particularly those tribes living in the Dent du Man mountain range. Here, on the high savannas, strong winds build up towards midday, posing a fire risk among the houses with thatched roofs. The function of the masquerader was to ensure that all cooking fires were extinguished before this time, and any woman failing to put her fire out before the masquerader came on his rounds had her cooking pots overturned and was beaten. The masks are distinguished by the application of red cloth or red pigment, clay, camwood powder or paint. The other categories of masquerade were the masquerade of the circumcision camp, the entertainment masquerade, the racing masquerade, the stilt-dancing masquerade, the dancing and miming masquerade, the symptom of illness masquerade and the judgement masquerade.

In addition to the life-size masks used in such masquerades, the Dan and other nearby tribes also carved miniature masks, measuring up to about 6in (15cm).

Guro, Ivory Coast, wood A unique and lively interpretation of an antelope, the zamle *is believed to have been created at the turn of the century.*

A miniature copy of a full-size mask might be carved by the owner of a mask to carry with him if he travelled away from home. In this way he could continue to communicate with the spirit and make any sacrifices that might be necessary. It might also serve the purpose of a 'passport' to identify to other groups his right to wear a particular type of mask. Unlike the use of full-size masks, the ownership of miniature masks was not a male preserve, and before she left home to marry, a girl might choose to commission a miniature copy of an important full-size mask belonging to her family. In such cases the small mask would be laid overnight with the larger prototype, after which sacrifices would be made. Miniature masks also served the purpose of witnesses to the proceedings in the circumcision camps.

To the south east of the Dan, the Ngere (or We) speak a different language but their culture resembles that of the Dan in many ways. Their masks have similarities to those of the Dan, but are more grotesque, with bulging cylindrical or slit eyes. A wide variety of materials are applied to the faces: horns, teeth, fur, bells, and even objects such as used rifle cartridge cases, which have been used to make beards. The masks of the Bete to the east are similar, but the tradition is believed to have been adopted from the Ngere only in the first quarter of the twentieth century.

The tribes of central Ivory Coast, such as the Baule, Guro and Yaure, produce masks in a style that is especially attractive to Western eyes and this no doubt explains the large quantity made today for the international art market. Human masks are the most notable in this respect, and among the Baule some are in

*Guro, Ivory Coast, wood
This mask (**above**)
exemplifies the typical
features of Guro human
masks, such as the slender
nose and small mouth.
However, the horn is an
unusual addition.
Height: 25in (63.5cm)*

*Baule, Ivory Coast, wood
The delicate features of the
Baule masks have an
obvious appeal to western
tastes and many copies of
masks of this type (**left**)
find their way onto the
market.
Height: 12¼in (31cm)
Christie's London 1988,
£4620*

*Yaure, Ivory Coast, wood
The zigzag border is a
common feature of Yaure
masks. As in this fine
example, the masks are
often more dramatic and
the expressions less sweet
than those masks of the
neighbouring Guro and
Baule tribes.
Height: 9in (23cm)*

fact portraits. For these, the carver would have to obtain permission from the subject, who would also have to be present when the mask was danced. Others represent general types such as 'prostitutes' or 'slaves'. Human masks are usually life-size, with small features, a slender nose, narrow slits to the eyes and a small mouth. It is often difficult to distinguish human masks of the Baule from those of the Yaure and Guro, but scarification and coiffure styles are helpful indicators.

Masks representing animals are also widely used. Some are carved in a naturalistic manner, clearly identifiable as buffalo, antelope or some other animal, but others are given human features and are distinguishable only by the addition of attributes such as horns. The masqueraders would appear one at a time in a series of entertaining sketches mimicking village life, starting with the least important characters, perhaps domestic animals, and finishing with important village personages. In the *Goli* masquerade, four pairs of masks were danced in order of importance, the least important being the distinctive *kple kple* mask. These are of simple design, the flat, circular face having a small, rectangular mouth with carved teeth. The eyes are carved as small projecting cones within a

painted lenticular- or drop-shape. The curved horns above almost join at the top to form a circle and are sometimes spirally carved. The face is blackened, with eyes and mouth embellished with white and red paint. They are usually no more than 18in (45cm) high, although some examples, perhaps made for the art market at a fairly early date, are much larger.

In the north of the Ivory Coast, in an area spanning the border of Mali and Burkina Faso, are the Senufo, who are closely related to the Dogon of Mali. They produce three main types of mask that the collector is likely to encounter. The most common of these is the *kpelie* mask, a female mask used principally as part of the ceremonies associated with the initiation of members into the *Poro* society. The face is of slender form, with narrow pierced eyes and a small mouth. Scarification marks are carved in relief. Almost invariably two curved 'legs' are carved from the bottom of the cheeks and represent hornbills—symbolic birds for the Senufo. The masks are surmounted by the horns of a ram or buffalo.

The most striking of Senufo masks is popularly known as the 'fire-spitter' and is again associated with

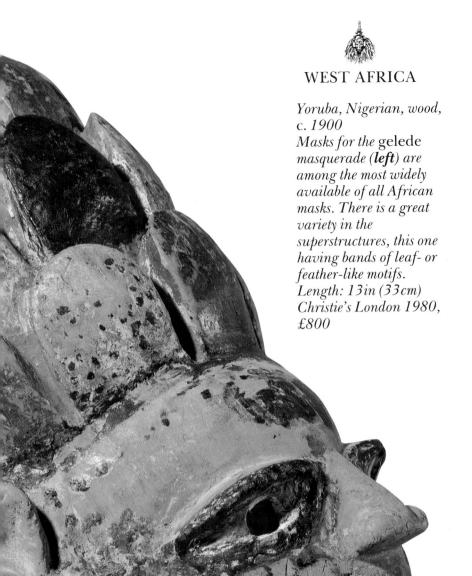

(left)

Yoruba, Nigerian, wood, c. 1900
Masks for the gelede *masquerade (**left**) are among the most widely available of all African masks. There is a great variety in the superstructures, this one having bands of leaf- or feather-like motifs.*
Length: 13in (33cm)
Christie's London 1980, £800

Senufo, Ivory Coast, wood
Kpelie *masks are characterized by horns projecting from the chin. They are frequently surmounted by a hornbill. This example (**above**) is unusual in having a panel of pointed projections.*

the *Poro* society. In fact, only a few of the Senufo groups use fire as part of the ritual associated with the masks, whether it be walking through fire or 'spitting' fire (by putting a few embers in the jaws), and masks rarely show any signs of scorching. The masks are of helmet form and combine features from various animals of symbolic value to the Senufo, such as horns of the bush cow, tusks of the wild boar, jaws of the crocodile, and a hornbill bird between the horns. Less common are masks of the type called *degele*. These consist of a simple unadorned helmet with a rectangular slit or two holes for the eyes. They are surmounted by a standing figure, sometimes carved in the typical manner of their figure sculpture, with tall crested coiffure, sometimes more stylized, and long

ringed neck or body, often without arms or legs.

On the border with Ghana are some groups that are influenced by Islam. Those known as the Ligbi produce masks somewhat resembling the Senufo *kpelie*, but with graceful rounded forms, the eyes pierced with curves. A group further north (on the border of Ghana and the Ivory Coast) produces masks up to 9ft (2.7m) tall, with the triangular face pierced with eyeholes surmounted by circular discs, supported by connecting struts and topped by horns. The earlier masks were smaller.

The Yoruba of south-west Nigeria are not only the largest tribe in Africa, but also probably the most prolific wood carvers. Masks are made for a number of societies and festivals, most notably the *Gelede* and *Egungun* societies and the *Epa* festival. The function of the *Gelede* secret society is to maintain the health

Yoruba, Nigeria, wood Two masks for the Epa *masquerade. The one on the left was acquired from the Church Missionary Society in 1935 and the one on the right was acquired from the Rev. Mr Lupton, to whom it was given by a missionary. Heights: 49¼in (125cm) and 51½in (131cm) Christie's London 1976, £2600 and £1300*

and prosperity of the community through plays and dances handed down from ancestors. The masqueraders always appear in pairs, one pair after another, and as many as 50 pairs, all different and each with its own name, might appear in quick succession at a single performance. Any male can carve the mask and dance in the *Gelede* masquerade, which is also said to placate the witchcraft in women.

The faces are naturalistically carved, normally having Yoruba facial characteristics; many show scarification marks on the cheeks, indicating the particular group to which they belong. Others may represent foreign characters; one popular character, 'the Brazilian', with white face, dark beard and hat, occurs around Lagos, which has long had a trading link with Brazil. Often in stark contrast to the serene faces of these masks, the coiffures, headdresses or superstructures show an immense variety of forms. Some have elaborate coiffures, others are carved with themes taken from all aspects of Yoruba life—groups of figures at work, domesticated animals, scenes from proverbs and so on. The eyes are usually pierced. This is not to enable the dancer to see (since the mask is worn on the top of the head), but rather is intended to add realism. The *Gelede* masquerade is held on the death of a member of the society and also in many towns in an annual festival.

The *Gelede* masquerade is practised only by the south-west Yoruba, in Nigeria and across the border in neighbouring Benin, but the *Egungun* masquerade is found throughout Yorubaland. The name *Egungun* means masquerade, though it is now used only to describe those ceremonies held to honour the ancestors. The cloth costume is of greater importance in *Egungun* ceremonies than is usual in most other African contexts; indeed it is sometimes danced with no mask, and it has been suggested that in these instances the characters may be of greater importance than those danced with a mask or headdress. The face masks are carved in a wide variety of styles and can often be confused with those from other areas. One which is easily recognizable, however, has a crest carved as a wooden head, with the hair carved as a long plait to one side of, and free of, the face. It is worn by a subgroup known as *Egungun layewu,* and is the privilege of the chief of hunters.

The most spectacular of Yoruba masks are found in north-east Yorubaland. These are the large helmet masks for the *Epa* festivals, held every two years in March and lasting for three days. The masks, measuring up to 5ft (1.5m) in height, are intended to be as large, unwieldy and elaborate as possible. The boys and young men who wear these masks have not only to dance, but also to jump onto a mound 3ft (1m) high, and for this the masqueraders must practise for months beforehand.

Yoruba, Nigeria, wood, metal
Similar to the gelede *masks, these are worn in the* Magbo *masquerade, a much rarer cult introduced from the neighbouring Ijo.*

Heights: 25¼in (64cm) and 18½in (47cm)
Christie's London 1986, £12,100 and £13,200

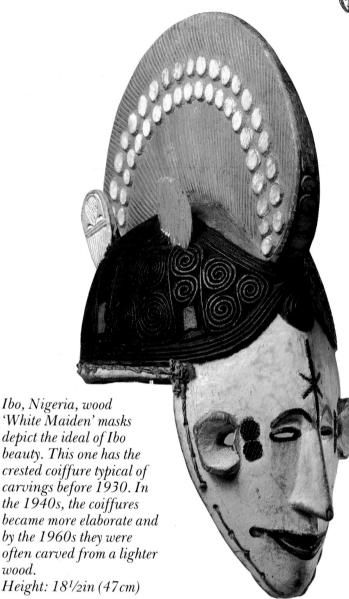

*Ibo, Nigeria, wood
'White Maiden' masks
depict the ideal of Ibo
beauty. This one has the
crested coiffure typical of
carvings before 1930. In
the 1940s, the coiffures
became more elaborate and
by the 1960s they were
often carved from a lighter
wood.
Height: 18½in (47cm)*

central region. The masqueraders are men belonging to the second of three age grades (that is, between the ages of about 30 and 50). They represent adolescent girls and embody the Ibo ideal of feminine beauty: pale complexion, straight slender nose and small mouth. The coiffures are moulded with clay, charcoal and oil into solid crests or other constructions decorated with bells, combs and similar ornaments. These highly elaborate styles were worn on masquerades celebrating special occasions, for example a marriage or the birth of a first child.

Mmwo masks would be worn with one of the most splendid of African masquerade costumes—a tight-fitting cloth outfit with appliqué geometric and floral patterns in red, green and other bright colours. The 'maidens' would be accompanied in their graceful dances by their sisters and mother, and occasionally an amusing contrast would be provided by an amorous, perhaps bawdy male masquerader.

To the south of the Ibo, the Ibibio (including the sub-groups Eket and Ogoni), though a much smaller tribe, are prolific carvers. Their principal society (*Ekpo*) is concerned with ancestor worship. Some masks have refined, naturalistic features with flowing curves, while others are more stylized and fierce, even grotesque. In the latter style, masks depicting faces ravaged and disfigured by tropical disease range in concept from a stark realism to more exaggerated representations of deformity, for example with the nose and mouth twisted in opposite directions. Keloids (raised scarification marks) are often prominent and the surface of the mask is usually blackened. A characteristic feature of Ogoni masks, by no means common elsewhere in Africa, is the articulated lower jaw, often inset with wooden teeth. This feature also occurs in Ibibio wooden puppets.

Masks carved by the tribes of the Benue Plateau and Upper Benue River have been collected only relatively recently, and much research has still to be published, but one can make the generalization that the masks from this area are among the most highly stylized of all Africa. The Mama carve headdresses of simplified form representing bush cows, with triangular snouts and stylized curved horns joined at the tips to form a circle. The most abstract of all African masks must be those of the Jukun. The Jukun were ruled by a divine king, the Aku of Wukari, who on accession was required to eat the brain, kidneys and heart of his predecessor, and was himself in turn strangled after seven years on the throne. One type of mask, known as *aku-onu*, consists of a concave oval, pierced with geometric shapes, said to represent a human head, with a conical projection at the back standing for the topknot worn by men on their otherwise shaven heads.

A highly distinctive group of masks and headdresses is found in the Cross River region of eastern Nigeria, spanning the border with Cameroon. Here the Ekoi (or Ejagham) carve headdresses and helmet masks of

The masks consist of a helmet carved as a grotesque face, with a large slit for the mouth, through which the dancer can see, surmounted by a disc (the entire mask is, however, carved from a single piece of wood). The large superstructure often consists of a chiefly figure, male or female, standing alone or sometimes surrounded by several attendants, all carved in the round, occasionally in several tiers. The principal mask of the *Epa* masquerade, however, depicts animals rather than humans. Known as *oloko*, it shows a leopard jumping onto the back of an antelope, surmounted by a cockerel. The ethnologist William Fagg, who was permitted to photograph several *Epa* masks at Ilofa, was told that the *oloko* could be brought out only if a dog were sacrificed.

To the east of the Yoruba, the Ibo are similarly large in number, but they live in much smaller communities—autonomous villages rather than large towns. The variety of masks produced by the Ibo and their neighbours is immense and only a few of the most popular and familiar can be mentioned here. Perhaps the type most likely to be encountered by collectors is the *mmwo* mask, danced in the annual 'fame of maidens' festival by the Ibo of the north

Ibo, Nigeria, wood
This highly abstract mask
(**above**) is a very rare type
of which few other
examples are known.
Height: 18⁷/₈in (48cm)
Christie's London 1980,
£2300

Ibibio, Nigeria, wood
This highly dramatic
mask (**right**) is a fine
example of the type
representing sufferers
from diseases or deformity.
This appears to represent a
sufferer with yaws, a
tropical skin disease most
notably affecting the nose.

*Bangwa, Cameroon, wood
This type of mask (**right**) is used by members of the 'night' society. Its use is restricted to an elite and it is seen only on rare occasions. Some later examples, on a much larger scale, were collected in about 1970.*

*Benin, Nigeria, bronze, copper, iron
There is no masking tradition at the court of Benin, the greatest kingdom in Nigeria. However, the oba or king of Benin wore bronze hip masks to secure his skirt-like drapery. The simple treatment of this ram's head (**left**) might indicate that it was cast in Owo, or in Benin by an Owo caster.
Height: 7⅞in (20cm)
Christie's London 1977, £3800*

*Cameroon grasslands, wood
The exotic headdresses of the chiefs or fons in the Cameroons grasslands are reflected in the superstructures of this mask (**right**). The headdresses would have been made of beaded fibre or cloth.
Christie's New York 1985, $17,600*

remarkable naturalism. The headdresses usually depict a head and neck, some larger than life-size, others smaller; examples carved as a whole figure are also known. The most notable feature of this group of masks is the antelope skin covering. Realism is enhanced by the addition of painted designs resembling tattoos and by the insertion of metal or wooden teeth, or occasionally by the addition of hair. Some examples represent young girls, their hair dressed in an extraordinary local ceremonial style of long spiral horns. It is said that originally these headdresses represented heads of enemies killed in local wars, and it has often been said by historians that early examples were covered in human skin; there does not seem to be any evidence to corroborate this, however, and intensive tests are needed to establish the identity of the skin once it has been treated and placed on the mask. Helmet masks are similarly covered in skin; some are carved in Janus form, with a pale-coloured female face and a dark male face, while others, more rarely, have as many as four faces. Skin-covered masks in the form of animal heads are said to represent animals killed during hunting expeditions.

The Cameroon grasslands are inhabited by numerous chieftaincies, some very small, ruled by a chief or *fon*. Social control is maintained by a regulatory society that, in each chieftaincy, owns a number of masks. Masks can also be owned by other groups, such as the society of princes, who were debarred from joining the regulatory society. The majority are human in character and larger than life-size. They may consist of just a face or be of helmet form. Despite the large number of chieftaincies, there is a unity of style evident in these masks. Usually they are carved with distinctive large eyes, which, as the mask is worn on top of the head, are not pierced; cheeks often bulge and ears stick out at the sides. The mouths are usually open and pierced with carved teeth, and white pigment is applied to teeth and eyes. The sex of the mask is generally not clear, but may be indicated by the type of coiffure. These can be very elaborate in themselves and may be carved with various animals associated with royalty, such as spiders and buffalo, often in a highly abstracted form.

Animal masks are also carved in a more naturalistic form, elephant masks having long straight trunks that project forward when the mask is worn on top of the head. More stylized elephant masks occur principally among the Bamileke and are worn by members of the *Kuosi* society, whose membership was limited to men

Kwele, Gabon, wood, early twentieth century
*This mask (**above**) has a whitened concave face typical of*
Kwele masks. Some examples are known with curving
horns framing the face and meeting below the chin.
Height: 24⅝in (62.5cm)

Mahongwe, Congo, wood, early twentieth century
*Only a few examples of this sort of mask (**above**) exist. A*
mask of this type was thought to have influenced Picasso's
painting Les Demoiselles d'Avignon.
Height: 14in (35.5cm)

of high rank who were able to pay the expensive entrance fees. These masks are made of cloth, sewn extensively with geometric designs in coloured glass beads, and have circular ears and a rectangular trunk that hangs loosely down the front of the wearer, who dresses in a voluminous indigo cloth outfit. They were worn at biannual festivals of the society and at funerals of both royalty and society members.

One of the finest of all African masks is the extremely rare type made by the Bangwa. No more than one such mask has been found in any single chieftaincy, which would seem to indicate their importance and their connection with royalty; their exact function, however, remains a mystery. Only 15 genuinely old examples are known to exist. The extraordinary conception, with the angled planes of cheeks and mouth and the tall, vertical structure above the eyes finely carved with parallel grooves, is highly individual. Some masks of this type, but larger than usual, were collected during the 1970s, and may have been made with an eye on the art market.

To the south, the Cameroon grasslands give way to dense, humid rain forest. Inhabitants of the area live in small villages of extended family units. The most famous tribe of the area is the Fang, best known for their reliquary figures—carved wood statues that are fixed to bark boxes or baskets containing the preserved bones of ancestors. They also produce several types of mask, although the original ceremonial purpose of many of these has been lost. Data of this kind is similarly lacking for many of the masks of the area, making precise attribution difficult. Helmet masks with up to six faces are used in ceremonies known as *Ngontang* (head of a young, white girl). The small whitened faces have small eyes and mouth, the wide brows curving towards the edge of the face to form a heart shape. Eyeholes for the wearer are carved below one of the faces. Single-face masks were made for the same ceremony and seem to pre-date the helmet variety. One such type is known through only a few examples, all of which are thought to date from about 1900. The whitened face has a slender nose, small eyes carved close together, and a small mouth, slightly open with carved teeth. The distinctive hairstyle is represented by a band of scorched triangles. At least one of these masks is carved with a moustache, which, together with the facial features, seems to indicate that they are intended to be representations of Europeans, who were becoming increasingly numerous in the area at the end of the nineteenth century.

The Fang society called *Ngil* is well known for the ritual executions that its members had to commit, a practice which, like the society itself, disappeared early in the country's colonial period. A type of mask, highly prized by collectors, is reputedly associated with *Ngil*, although there seems to be little evidence to support the connection. The masks are large, sometimes more than 3ft (1m) long, and are whitened with kaolin. The

*Fang, Gabon, wood
The Fang invariably
whiten their masks with
kaolin: this example
(**above**) may have been
intended to represent a
European.
Height: 15½in (39.5cm)
Christie's New York 1984,
$24,200*

*Fang, Gabon, wood
Mission stations
commissioned masks from
traditional carvers in
Gabon for sale to
Europeans. These were
usually single-faced
masks, and helmet masks
such as this (**left**) are more
likely to have been carved
for traditional purposes.
This example was formerly
in the collection of André
Breton.
Height: 13⅜in (34cm)*

narrow heart-shaped face has a long, slender nose and the small eyes and mouth are scorched. The function of the execution rituals within *Ngil* society was to punish social deviants.

To the east of the Fang, and related to them, are the Kwele. Few artefacts by them are known, but the majority are masks. Little is known about their use; some show no evidence of having been worn and may simply have been displayed on ceremonial occasions. Those of human form generally have small heart-shaped faces and small mouths (although the mouth is sometimes omitted altogether). The eyes are raised, with narrow slits that are not always pierced—one of the reasons for thinking that not all were intended to be worn. Faceted horns on some masks curve about

the face; they sometimes meet below and frame the face, and they may be carved with small faces or eyes. The Kwele also make animal masks, representing gorillas, antelopes and elephants. Antelopes are of simplified geometric form, with lozenge-shaped faces echoed in the lozenge shape formed by the horns above. Elephant masks have faces resembling those of the human masks, but are carved with a faceted trunk curving down from the top of the head.

To the south of the Kwele, the Kota and Mahongwe are famous for their brass-covered reliquary figures. The Mahongwe also made a style of mask now very rare (there may be no more than four old examples in existence today), with a concave face tapering to a point at the chin. The forehead is prominent and the eyes are raised, with pierced slits. The nose is triangular and the mouth small and conical.

A number of related tribes along the Ngunie River in southern Gabon produce a type of mask that is without doubt the most famous of all Gabonese masks. This is the white-faced mask made by the Punu and related tribes such as the Lumbo. The earliest known example was collected in 1867 and is now in the Pitt-Rivers Museum in Oxford. They gained popularity in the 1920s and 1930s, when many arrived in Europe, sadly with no collection data. As a result, precise attribution has been made difficult, if not impossible. They have been said to represent female ancestors and were worn in the *Okuni* masquerade, in which the dancer performed acrobatic feats on tall stilts. The masks, with serene expressions, are whitened with kaolin and have reddened lips. The eyes have curved narrow slits and the overall effect is remarkably reminiscent of Japanese female faces or masks. On most examples the blackened coiffure has a tall central lobe flanked by two lower lobes, and keloids are frequently carved in relief on the centre of the forehead, usually a group of nine forming a lozenge.

To the south of Gabon, across the border and into the People's Republic of the Congo, are the Teke. Only the eastern Teke, known as the Tsaye, produce masks, called *kidumu*. Their masking tradition is believed to have commenced only in the nineteenth century, and few of the surviving masks are thought to date from before the start of the twentieth century. The masks are circular (some of the late examples are oval) and flat, divided horizontally by a ridge at the level of the top of the nose. All of them, not surprisingly, are vertically symmetrical, but two of the oldest examples are also horizontally symmetrical. The masks are incised with geometric designs and painted in colours, usually black, white and red or orange. Two symbolic traditions are said to exist—one of them political, featuring crocodiles, crossroads, moons, pythons and rainbows, the other more generalized, with moons, sun, stars and rainbow. Sometimes these motifs suggest a resemblance to a face, but this is said to be a trick designed to mislead the uninitiated. The masks are pierced about the border for the attachment of feathers and raffia fibres. It is thought that production of these masks ceased in about 1920 and was revived only in the past 20 years or so, some of the modern artists relying for their inspiration on western books on African art.

EQUATORIAL AFRICA

The Portuguese explorer Diego Cao first reached the mouth of the Zaire (or Congo) River in the 1480s and found here the flourishing Kongo kingdom, with complex political institutions and social life. The Kongo kingdom maintained close contact with Portugal from the fifteenth century, notably for the trade in ivory and slaves. Many upper-class Kongo were

Kongo, Zaire, wood
*Masks from the area of the mouth of the Congo River such as this one (**right**) are among the most naturalistic of all African interpretations of the human face, but are scarce.*

Teke-Tsaye, Zaire, wood
*Few old examples of this type of mask (**above**) are known to exist. Many were collected in the 1950s, or later, when the tradition was revived.*
Christie's London 1980, £6600

Punu, Gabon, wood
*The tribes along the Ogowe River all carved masks with a somewhat oriental appearance (**right**); the scarification and the coiffure vary from one example to the next.*
Christie's London 1987, £7700

Pende, Zaire, wood and raffia
*The masquerades of the Pende include a large number of characters who wear similar types of mask (**right**) and examples are readily available on the market.*
Length: 23⅝in (60cm)
Christie's London 1978, £3600

Lega, Zaire, wood and fibre
*Lega masks are made in various sizes and, like this one (**above**), are usually carved in wood, although they can also be ivory or elephant hide. The Bwami society still exists, and it is often difficult to tell the age of a mask.*
Height: approx. 6in (15cm)

converted to Christianity, and Portuguese members were among the group of governors who elected the king, or *ntotela*, to office. Not surprisingly, European influence, particularly Christian themes, are evident in the art of the area from an early date. The most famous carvings from the area are large nail fetish figures and small wooden maternity figures.

Various tribes were dominated by the Kongo or came within their sphere of influence. Of these, the Woyo and the Yombe produce masks. The Woyo, who live on the west coast, north of the estuary of the Zaire River, use masks known as *ndunga*, which are still made and danced today in ceremonies associated with initiation. The masks are larger than life-size, with projecting foreheads, swelling cheeks and narrow pierced eyes. The mouths are open, with carved teeth. The surface is painted either white or in colours, often in an asymmetrical design of broad areas of colour speckled with spots. The masks of the Yombe, to the north, are much rarer and little is known about their use. They display a much greater degree of realism than those of the Woyo and are life-size.

To the south-west, both in Zaire and across the border in Angola, are the Yaka and Suki, who live in an area of sparsely populated savanna. They share institutions concerning leadership and divination, and their art, which is relatively well documented, has many similarities. Both tribes have initiation schools (like the *Poro* of west Africa) in which the youths are circumcised and taught various skills, songs and dances. Various masks are used in connection with the accompanying ceremonies. Helmet masks, known as *hemba*, are predominantly used by the Suku. These usually have a whitened face with blackened incised coiffure, which is often surmounted by a bird, animal or figure. Examples carved since 1930 also have a handle carved below the chin.

Among the northern Yaka is made a series of masks said to represent departed elders, the most elaborate of which is called *kholuka*. These have a small face with bulging eyes and an open mouth with carved teeth. One of the most distinctive features of the masks is the nose, which is always prominent and often turns sharply upwards, a characteristic often seen in the figure sculpture from the same area. The headgear is made of raffia cloth and is frequently conceived as a cone, with one or more horizontal flanges or upward curved projections. The flanges and prongs denote the grade and are specified by the society, while the wooden mask can be carved to the whim of the man who commissions it. This headgear is sometimes surmounted by a figure or figures, frequently featuring sexuality and procreation in both humans and animals. On others, items associated with domestic activity are shown, or they may be topped by mammals, birds, fish or reptiles. Among both the Suku and the Yaka a type of very large mask is made averaging almost 3ft (1m) in height. Known as *kakuungu*, they were sup-

ported by a vertical handle from the chin, hidden in performance behind the raffia fringe. They have bulging cheeks and chin and a projecting, pouting mouth. The face is painted with red and white pigment.

The Western Pende, to the east of the Suku on the upper Kwilu River in Zaire, live in numerous chiefdoms of varying size. Ancestors, who are at the root of all Pende religion, are worshipped in shrines and make themselves visible at masquerades. There are two types of masks: *minganji*, which are the more powerful, represent ancestors, while *mbuya* are village masks representing various character types, such as chief, executioner, fool, flirt and prostitute. There are as many as 20 types, although only a few appear in any one ceremony. The performances are entertaining and amusing, but also a means of effecting social control. The *mbuya* masks usually have a triangular-shaped face, with half-closed, bulging eyes and eyebrows carved in relief meeting at the centre above the nose; mouths are often open with carved teeth. Some characters have a long, rectangular beard curving out below the chin and carved with grooves. The masks are painted in various colours, usually black, white and red; the epileptic, *mbangu*, has a face painted half black and half white.

The more forceful *minganji* masks, representing ancestors, are of simpler form. They are circular and made from plaited raffia, with tubular eyes and no other facial features. All mask manufacture is a sacred process that must not be seen by women and children, who are permitted to view them only in the masquerade; consequently masks are carved away from the village. *Mbuya* dancers in *Makenda* circumcision ceremonies emerge from the bush one at a time and dance in the village square from afternoon until dusk, at which time the *minganji* masqueraders appear, but only at a distance. They rush around on the outskirts of the village but never enter it, and they make themselves only partly visible to the spectators, thus adding to the sense of awe and fear they are intended to create. At the conclusion of the ceremony, the masqueraders remove their masks in the presence of the newly initiated youths at the circumcision camps, who are then allowed to touch and handle the masks and are thus acknowledged as equals.

Small versions of these masks, measuring approximately 2–2½in (5–6cm) in height, are carved in ivory or wood and are worn as amulets. Ivory examples often acquire a fine smooth surface and golden colour much admired by collectors. European fakers are becoming increasingly skilled at reproducing these characteristics and giving them just the right amount of 'wear' around the suspension holes. Small wooden masks, measuring about 2½–4in (6–10cm), are carved as oracles and are fixed to the end of a concertina of wooden sticks, like a jack-in-the-box. They are pierced about the top of the head for the attachment of a feather coiffure.

The eastern Pende produce a number of regional mask styles. One of these, the *giphogo*, forms part of the chief's treasury. It is a cylindrical helmet mask, with almond-shaped slit eyes and a projecting cylindrical nose. Below the chin is a wide flange carved and painted with bands of triangles. The name *giphogo* is also applied to another type of mask surmounted by two sword-like projections.

The Kuba kingdom incorporates almost 20 different tribes, the Bushoong and Kete being the largest. The Kuba live in Zaire in the fork of the Kasai and Sankuru rivers. Art and masks play an important role in court ritual, initiation and funerals. A number of related masks, used in dances re-enacting the origins of the Kuba kingdom, are made from a combination of several materials. The most important of these masks among the Bushoong is called *moshambwooy*, which has the following legendary origin. A water spirit once haunted the country, inflicting blindness and fatal illnesses on the inhabitants. In the time of the king Bo Kyeen, a man called Bokomboke met the spirit in the forest. Frightened, he returned to the village and recounted to the king what he had seen, but was unable to describe the being in words. The king ordered him to build a hut on the edge of the village, and with some barkcloth, the skin of a bat and feathers he made a strange costume, which he painted in yellow, black and white. The king saw the costume and had an idea. He disappeared for so long that people wondered what had happened to him. One night, a strange being appeared in the capital. Wearing a costume imitating the spirit *moshambwooy*, it was the king frightening the inhabitants. Then the king hid the costume in the bush. Next day the king reappeared and expressed great astonishment at the story of the visit of the strange being, but claimed to know the reason for the stranger's visit. It was *moshambwooy* come to see if there were any querulous women or disobedient youths to be punished.

The face of the mask is usually of leopard or antelope skin, to which a wooden mouth and nose are attached. Cowrie shell eyes are surrounded by glass beads, and a panel of beads with chevron or zigzag designs runs down the centre of the face. A chevron at the bottom of the face represents a beard and is sewn with rows of cowrie shells. The mask is supported and strengthened by a rigid crown of rattan sewn all over with beads, which also serves to hold in place the raffia cloth head covering. This is also sewn extensively, with coloured beads forming interlocking geometric designs; such designs are typical of the Kuba and are seen also in wood carving and scarification patterns. The mask is worn with a highly elaborate costume made from similar materials and is surmounted by a crown of feathers. A number of masks are similar in appearance to the *moshambwooy* and are sometimes confused with it. *Mukyeem* may have served a similar function and differs from the *moshambwooy*

Kuba, Zaire, wood, raffia, cloth, cowries and metal
A number of tribes within the Kuba kingdom made elaborate masks from a wide variety of materials;
Moshambwooy *masks (**above**) are the most elaborate. Height: 17³⁄₄in (45cm) Christie's London 1989, £462*

Salampasu, Zaire, wood, feathers, fibre and rattan
*The form of the Salampasu mask (**right**) is very distinctive with rounded forehead, small rectangular mouth and triangular face. Height: 30³⁄₈in (77cm)*

in having a trunk-like projection from the top of the head, a feature which is derived from the trunk of an elephant, a symbol of power.

Various explanations have been given for the origin of the mask known as *bwoom*, which sometimes appears alongside *moshambwooy*. One is that it represents a pygmy, another that it represents the hydrocephalous head of the son of a fourteenth-century king. The wooden mask is of helmet form and has a prominent forehead and large nose. The forehead, cheeks and mouth are usually covered with sheets of copper and again the surface is extensively embellished with beads and cowrie shells.

The female mask, *ngady amwaash*, also appears

Chokwe, Zaire, wood, fibre, glass beads and metal
This impersonation of female beauty, called mwana pwo, *is worn by a masquerader on stilts. Shown in profile (**right**) and face-on (**far right**), this is a very fine example of the most widely available of all Chokwe masks; however, the quality can vary considerably. Large quantities were made at the Dundo Museum in Angola.*

alongside *moshambwooy* and *bwoom*. It is a face mask of wood and, compared with other Kuba masks, is of fairly naturalistic form. A vertical panel of beads runs down the length of the nose and mouth and the eyebrows are also beaded, but the remainder of the face is painted with bold geometric designs in black and white. The attached raffia headgear is sewn with cowries and painted with geometric designs.

To the south of the Kuba the Bena Biombo produce helmet masks showing the clear influence of the Pende to the west and Kuba to the north. The face is reddened and the cheeks and chin are carved and painted with bands of triangles in black and white.

Slightly further south, the Salampasu make masks in both wood and fibre. The wooden masks have prominent bulging foreheads and pointed chins, large apertures for the eyes and rectangular pierced mouths with carved and whitened pointed teeth. On some masks copper panels are attached to the surface. Frequently the coiffure is represented by balls of woven cane, and similar balls may be suspended from the chin on lengths of plaited fibre to represent a beard. Masks were also made from woven fibre, resembling the wooden masks in having bulging forehead and similar eye apertures. These masks also sometimes have the cane ball coiffures, or alternatively, are topped with woven fibre or feathers. Although the Salampasu are said to have destroyed their masks in

the early 1960s, partly in an effort to move into contemporary life, it was reported in 1975 that mask production had increased to meet a growing demand, no doubt from the art market.

The Lwalwa are related to the Salampasu and at one time were under their domination. They produce four types of similar mask; they have concave, almost lozenge-shaped faces, with reddened patina, sometimes embellished with white. Three are male and one female. Eyes are rectangular slits and mouths are small and project forward. The male *nkaki* mask has a long, prominent and slender nose extending to the top of the forehead, and *shifola* masks, also male, have shorter, rounded noses. The female mask, *mushika*, is distinguished by a lateral crest to the coiffure, and noses are generally less pronounced. The fourth type, *mvondo*, also male, has a nose similar to the female mask, but does not have the crested coiffure.

There are three categories of mask used by the Chokwe, who live on the border of Angola and Zaire. The most important are sacred masks called *cikungu*, worn by chiefs at their enthronement and while making certain sacrifices. Made of black resin on a wooden frame, they have large circular discs for ears, a stylized chin and a large elaborate headgear. They are painted with geometric designs in red and white. There are various types of circumcision masks, also with resin faces, though with less pronounced features. *Cikungu*,

Mbunda, Zambia, wood
Influenced by their Chokwe neighbours, Mbunda masks
(**above**) *have clear affinities with Chokwe masks although*
they are larger and rarer.
Height: 13¾in (35cm) Christie's London 1989, £4620

the most important of these, has a tall conical superstructure, sometimes over 3ft (1m) high, representing
the horns of the roan antelope and with a series of
rings representing the rings of growth. These masks
are usually destroyed after the initiation ceremonies
have taken place, and they are therefore unlikely to
be encountered by the collector.

The most familiar Chokwe masks are the dance
masks, which are kept by professional dancers, who
destroy them only if they are damaged. Dancing is a
hereditary occupation handed down from uncle to
nephew. There are two principal types of masks: the
cihongo, which is male, and the more common *pwo*,
which is female. Both types are made in resin and
wood. The *cihongo* is approximately life-size, with slit
almond-shaped eyes within concave sockets. The
pierced mouth is broad, with carved whitened teeth;
the chin is stylized, represented by a projecting disc.
The forehead is usually incised with a scarification
mark called *cingelyengelye*, shaped like a Maltese cross.
The mask represents the male ancestor and symbolizes power and wealth, the virile dance contrasting to
the elegance of the female (though the two were rarely, if ever, performed together).

The female mask, *pwo* or *mwana pwo* (young woman),

Songye, Zaire, wood
Height: 20⅞in (53cm)
Christie's London 1989, £3850

*Songye, Zaire, wood, fibre and
feathers
Height: 18¹/8in (46cm)
Christie's New York 1984, $33,000*

represents the female ancestor and imparts fertility to the spectators. These masks are more naturalistic than the *cihongo* masks, and although they represent the female ancestral spirit, some have the appearance of portraits. The faces are reddened and usually have a serene expression. The artist is said to be inspired by the looks of a particularly beautiful woman, and since he has to work far away from women, he studies his model at length, often for several days, to imprint her features on his mind. Eyes are frequently represented in a similar way to those on *cihongo* masks, but the mouth, which may be open or closed, is smaller. The dancer is dressed as a woman, with false breasts. The solemn bearing and elegant gestures of the *pwo* masks are said to teach the Chokwe women to act in a graceful manner. The Chokwe also carve masks representing animals such as pigs, monkeys and guinea fowl.

To the south of the Chokwe, on the borders of Angola and Zambia, are the Mbunda. They are related to the Chokwe and make large wooden masks, over life-size, which have a distinctive large rectangular mouth, often with carved teeth. The forehead is very prominent and is sometimes carved with curved parallel grooves. Some masks have bulging cheeks reminiscent of masks from the Cameroon grasslands.

Probably the most striking masks from Zaire are the *kifwebe* masks of the Songye and Luba, highly distinctive because of their cubistic forms and vibrant painted decoration. Writers disagree as to which tribe adopted the style from the other. There is considerable stylistic variation, but the masks usually have a square jaw and rectangular mouth projecting to the same distance as the nose. A median crest of varying height runs from the top of the head, often linking up with the nose (though this is absent or very shallow on female masks). The eyes frequently have large projecting hoods. Most of the masks are incised and painted with bands of alternating colours, the most common being black, white and red. Generally speaking, those masks with very exaggerated features are later in date. Among the Luba, whose kingdom dominated and influenced a wide area of south-west Zaire, *kifwebe* masks of similar style are carved in the east. This region is also associated with masks of hemispherical form, with similar surface decoration of parallel grooves, in this case usually painted white on a black ground, and with large helmet masks of rounded form. The features are more naturalistic than on the *kifwebe* masks and the surface is blackened. Some of these, though of human form, have curved horns.

To the east of the Luba, and closely related to them, are the Hemba. Although best known for their figure sculpture, the Hemba also make small masks representing chimpanzees, with wide grinning, crescent-shaped mouths and narrow eyes. These masks usually have a dark crusty patina. Called *soko mutu*, or *soko muntu*, they were probably not intended to be worn

PACIFIC MASKS

Like the masks of many African cultures, those of Melanesia reflect a strong tradition of ceremonial masquerades and religious rituals. Probably the strongest thematic link between the various cults is the importance accorded to tribal ancestors, whose benevolent spirits are frequently invoked.

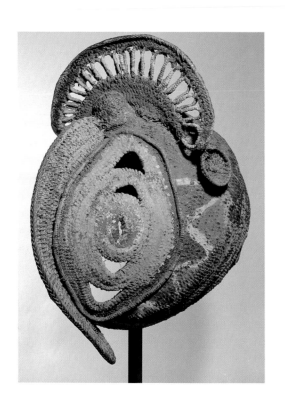

The islands of the South Pacific, collectively known as Oceania, are divided into three major groups: Melanesia, Micronesia and Polynesia. In Micronesia and Polynesia masks are virtually unknown, but in the larger islands of Melanesia the situation is completely different, for these islands are a treasure house of masks, comparable to Africa for variety and artistic quality. Much of the old tradition is as strong as ever, and many of the masquerades are still being danced today.

MELANESIA

Although many of the peoples of Melanesia are confessed Christians of one denomination or another, they practise many of the old rites, and most of the churches recognize the value of leaving those bonds of society intact, provided they are denuded of any destructive elements. Masks play a vital and prominent part in these peoples' lives. They do not view the supernatural from the same standpoint as a European, but as an extension of the everyday world. The most powerful and influential spirits are generally held to be those of important ancestors, and particular atten-

tion is paid to the proper performance of mortuary and funerary rites at the passing of men of high status. Spirits are potentially either malevolent or benevolent and human actions can placate or aggravate them. Societies were created to control, direct and modify their power, and the feasts given to appease them and to venerate the ancestors were linked with initiation rites of boys and young men.

The masks used at such ceremonies are sometimes abandoned afterwards, but others are kept for years;

Maprik, New Guinea, basketry, twentieth century
*Used in dances connected with the yam cult, masks such as this (**above left**) come in a variety of forms and sizes. They are abandoned after the ceremony, and are widely available on the market today.*

Unea Island, barkcloth, various fibres, cane and feathers
*These rare large conical fibre masks (**right**) are painted in striking, bright colours.*
Height: 27½in (70cm)

the former are usually available on the market, but when the latter appear for sale they may have been acquired illegally. This fact accounts in part for the importance that many collectors attach to provenance. The acquisition of a mask or other work of art is usually channelled through the headman of a village. Some collectors have had the galling experience of paying for an artefact, only to have it wrested from them when the indignant, real owner suddenly and unexpectedly appears.

Some parts of Melanesia have been accessible for well over a century, but others, because of the difficult terrain or inhospitable climate are little explored even today. New Guinea is the largest and best-known island in Melanesia and it also has the richest artistic traditions. The most prolific area for masks is probably the vast valley of the Sepik River, especially along the middle and lower reaches, where the waters flow from west to east in great lazy loops. Ceremonies are centred on the men's meeting houses, called *Tambaran*—huge thatched buildings with upturned eaves to each end, and a tall decorated front. Inside, the most sacred masks and figures are stored from ceremony to ceremony (the dancing takes place on the dance floor nearby). The masks of the middle Sepik are usually made of wood or woven split cane, rattan, or a mixture of both. Some large conical masks extend to below the waist of the wearer, so that he puts his arms through two holes at the sides. Often a further mask of wood or clay is attached both before the face and at the summit of the cone; the clay masks are embellished with cowrie shell eyes and bands of small nassa shells are usually inset about the rim. Other rattan masks can be woven as animals, chiefly crocodiles.

All the ceremonies need the beneficial presence of the ancestors, and celebrate the emergence of the initiates from their seclusion, fortified by their trials and grown from boys into men. Among the Maprik, who live in a mountainous area to the north of the middle Sepik, the ceremonies are centred about the cultivation of yams, and the rattan masks are painted in bright colours—bands of red, yellow, black and white, sometimes also green. They vary in size from huge hemispherical constructions that engulf the torso of the masquerader to small ones, less than 12in (30cm) high, which are used to decorate the enormous yams grown especially for the feasts. After the ceremonies most of the masks are abandoned in the forest, so this type of mask is readily available on the market. Woven rattan masks are made by other groups in this area, and are painted in earth colours of reddish-brown, black and white, with sometimes a little green. The colours fade and some masks are repainted for each performance.

Further downstream, near Anggoram, the people use large, oval, dish-like masks attached to rattan. This type of mask has proved popular with collectors and many are made today for the art market. Similar masks

Sepik River, wood, shell and fibre
*The slender oval face and hooked nose (**above**) is typical of masks from the lower Sepik River area. Christie's London 1979, £2200*

*Papuan Gulf, cane and barkcloth (**right**)*

are carved in the Sepik Delta area and up the Ramu river, some of the masks having long, thin noses in a rather long oval face.

The wooden masks of the Yuat river, a tributary of the Sepik, are of rather bulbous form, usually the size of a human face. They are painted in colours, predominantly white, red and yellow, over areas indicated in relief, and have rather aggressive features. Masks from the Ramu, Murik Lakes and the Sepik Delta are usually covered in a reddish mud paste and sometimes have an animal carved in high relief on the forehead and a long, looped nose. A 'classic' type of Sepik mask, the oval about the size of a human face, and with typical scrolls carved at intervals about the border and features, is carved on Manam Island, just off the north coast of New Guinea, and is traded to neighbouring islands as well as to other villages along the coast. Such masks are still carved today with great precision, and it takes a well-trained eye to pick out the old ones from the new.

Wooden masks from Irian Jaya, the north-western promontory of New Guinea, are rare and show the influence of neighbouring Indonesian islands. The Asmat to the south have knotted fibre masquerading costumes that cover the whole body. Their masks are roughly conical, painted reddish-brown and white, with applied round eyes of wood and a woven nose with a wooden nose ornament attached. At the top of the head is inserted a stick with pendants of white feathers and seed pods from the plant called Job's tears. Even further south are the people of Marind Anim, who wear very elaborate constructions of sago palm trunk, with applied abrus seeds, shell ornaments and feathers; many similarly decorated panels are worn about the whole figure, making a vast and colourful assemblage.

Some of the finest New Guinea masks come from the Gulf of Papua on the south coast, an area of river deltas and mud flats. They are made of bark cloth stretched over a cane frame, the black and white designs outlined by further applications of split cane and surmounted by tall oval panels decorated with stylized faces and figures. All masks from this area have a conical base to enclose the head, with the eyes embellished with a forked motif. Above this cone are attached large oval panels (typical of the western part of the Gulf) or bird and fish forms (found further east along the Gulf).

The final main masking area of New Guinea is in the north-east, from Astrolabe Bay to the Huon Gulf. In this area are carved rather heavy wooden masks, painted with designs in red, black and white; apart from their rectangular form, they are recognizable by the forked decoration about the eyes and the large, often looped, ear lobes. A round mask, called *tago*, of palm spathe topped by a bunch of cassowary feathers, is also made in this area and painted similar colours.

The Torres Straits, to the south of New Guinea, are

*Witu Island, wood
This wooden helmet mask (**above**) is of a type rarely available on the market.
Height: 20in (51cm)
Christie's London 1980,
£6000*

*Tami Island, Papua New Guinea, barkcloth, feathers, fibre and shells
This particular type of barkcloth mask (**left**) is known as* tago

47

scattered with small islands, on most of which are constructed tortoiseshell masks of great complexity. Panels of shell from the local turtles are pared down and cut into the necessary shapes and sewn together with plaited coconut fibre to make long masks, worn at an angle on the heads of the masqueraders. A smaller mask, the size of a human head, is often applied on the forehead of the larger mask, which can incorporate monstrous features. Cassowary feathers are inserted about the fretted borders, large conus and other shells are suspended about the rim, and long wooden prongs with inserted white feathers form a crest. Occasionally the crest is of fish form. The initiates were taken for several weeks to a secret camp in the bush, where they were taught the myths and legends, dances and rites relating to the culture heroes. The dances were performed at night before a screen hung with shells, skulls and effigies. The masqueraders, representing the mythic ancestors, wore long grass costumes beneath the masks, and were seen by the initiates alone. Later the initiates, having passed all the tests, were bathed, painted and dressed, then taken back to the main camp, where they were greeted as though returned from the dead, re-united with their families and made ready for marriage. Few of these splendid masks have survived intact; but in the small masks that are attached to the larger ones the particular process of creative thinking is still evident, and even stripped to the minimum of just the oval face with the attached looped nose, some of the mystic element is retained. On Saibai Island, just off the coast of New Guinea, are carved long wooden masks, with an eye form similar to the others of the Torres Straits, with inset hair and beard, and incised, painted borders.

About 100 miles (160km) to the east of New Guinea, across the Siassi Sea, is the island of New Britain. Some masks there are similar to those made on New Guinea, but in the far east of the island—in the Gazelle Peninsula—masks of a dramatically different kind are produced. They are used in mourning ceremonies, to commemorate those who had died during the previous year, and to celebrate the ripening of the taro harvest; this represented a ritual continuation or activation of a pattern of cyclical change of birth, growth and death of all living things. One type of mask, called *hareiga,* is truly gigantic, being some 30-40ft (9-12m) high, and is carried to the dance area by a large group of men. It is constructed of barkcloth over a cane frame, with a round or ovoid head, the features painted in black, on a long, thin neck, a small body below. Such huge objects naturally tend to find their way into museums rather than private collections. The best examples are in German museums, especially that at Bremen, where clustered in a corner, they are awe-inspiring.

There are several types of smaller headdress masks, similarly constructed and painted, but none is still made today. Large composite helmet masks known as *oggeroggeruk* are, however, produced today; indeed,

Torres Straits, Papua New Guinea, turtleshell, shells, fibre, feathers
Turtleshell was rarely used for masks outside the Torres Straits (between the south of New Guinea and the northern tip of Australia). Masks from this region command high prices at auction. They are more usually of human form, and this fish mask (**left**) is particularly rare.

Baining, Gazelle Peninsula, New Britain, cane and barkcloth
Several different types of barkcloth masks are used in the area of the Gazelle Peninsula in the east of New Britain. Some are of immense size and are consequently rarely seen on the market. The pig mask (**above**) is one of several animals represented in barkcloth masks danced at night.

Sulka, New Britain, wood, various fibres
Masks from central New Britain are among the most dramatic of Melanesian masks. Delicacy and fragility no doubt partly account for their relative scarcity on the market today. Several examples were collected at the beginning of the century, the majority of which are to be found in German museums.

the tradition they serve seems to have originated in its present form only in the twentieth century. These masks, said to symbolize the slow growth of trees, have a long, slightly-tapered, cylinder with a curious face at the end, just above the dancer's head. They are sometimes found on the market today, as are examples of a type of mask danced at night. Again, these are made of barkcloth over a rattan or cane frame, and painted with black designs. They fit over the dancer's head and resemble to a greater or lesser degree the creatures they are said to represent—the owl, hornbill, flying fox, pig, cow and fish.

Similar masks from the central Baining area of the island are made for another night dance, known as the Baining snake dance. Two types, called *kavat* and *vungvung*, are still made today in the area. The *kavat* masks have a distinctive iconography, depicting various flora, birds, mammals, insects, reptiles, natural phenomena and human processes and products. Typical features include *slabam* ('vertebrae of a pig'), *saulki* ('support post of a house'), *rengit* ('leaf used for wrapping food for cooking') and *surraga* ('wise old man'). Older masks have fine negative designs painted in black on the natural barkcloth, but later types are more simply decorated, concentrating on huge eyes painted in red and black with concentric circles.

Sulka, New Britain, wood, fibres
There is a great variety in the Sulka masks. This one clearly represents a human figure. Others are made as huge discs worn on top of the head and resembling umbrellas. The painted decoration is usually in the favoured colours of pink and green.

The mask made today in the largest quantities has huge round eyes within a lobed structure, which tapers above the rounded jaws; a lip or tongue-like protrusion hangs below the jaw and the structure extends at the back to fit on the head of the dancer. The whole creation can be about 3ft (1m) high, but smaller ones are made, probably with a view to export. As they come leaping out of the forest at night, they make a stirring impression, even if they do have a certain resemblance to Mickey Mouse and Donald Duck.

The Tolai people in the Tolai mountains, also in the north-east of New Britain, have two types or families of mask. The first is the *dukduk*, a high composite cone with a long waving topknot. *Dukduks* are thought of as the 'sons' of conical palm spathe masks with large circular painted eyes. (Some authorities believe they are rather the male and female types of the same masking tradition.) The latter are made today in a number of different materials—cotton cloth, mosquito netting, printed cloth or anything similar that is available. These cones are perched above an enveloping tiered leaf robe. The 'mother' of both these masks is said to dwell in the Duke of York Islands, to the east, but she does not accompany the *dukduks* and their 'mothers' when they arrive on the beach in their

canoes. Having arrived by sea, the *dukduks* and their mothers dance on the beach and enter the village only to take food. Although they are in fact men from that village, when masquerading they have the absolute right to take whatever they wish—fruit, yams, even a small pig—to be eaten by the elders and the young initiates. The masks are highly sacred and it is forbidden for the people to sell them. They are also extremely frail, and consequently are seldom found on the market, or even in museums.

The same is true of the other type of mask made by the Tolai. This consists of a hemisphere of rattan, covered in ferns or other fibres, with a triangular wooden face attached to one side; this in turn often has a fibre beard, feathers about the neck, pierced nose ornaments and bright painted decoration (all the colours used are made from natural materials, except the blue, which is a bleach bought at the trade stores). On the top of this structure can be attached a wooden figure, usually about 18in (45cm) high, finely-carved and with animated stance. This also is brightly coloured, and often embellished with thorns, intricately-applied eyes and inset fibre hair; it stands within three or four finely-serrated wooden cascades curving from a pole above the head to the circular platform at the base. These two elements, the figure and the mask, are stored in separate huts, and must never be seen by women, especially when joined together for the dance, when their potency is comparable to lightning or an electric charge. It is probably because of this method of storage that the mask is seldom collected whole, and even in museums the figures have often been separated from the faces.

Along the coast of the Gazelle Peninsula is found a mask made from a human skull, minus the jaw, with a mud and gum encrustation, inset hair, and a small stick at the back with which to hold it in the dancer's teeth. Then to the south of the peninsula is found another group of highly dramatic masks, among the most spectacular made anywhere in the world—fantastical structures made of rattan, covered in pith, and then painted a variety of pinks, bright greens, black and white. Although the basic mask is of conical or truncated cylindrical form, the superstructures can resemble vast umbrellas, with the eyes separated on stalks and other features stylized or exaggerated. In addition to traditional materials, the makers of the masks use wire, cotton cloth, paper, cardboard, netting or whatever else may be to hand. Inset feathers are used, as everywhere in Melanesia, and the masqueraders show great imagination with their inventions. The celebrations continue all day and all night for several days, after which the masks are abandoned in the forest. It is not always easy to tell what characters the dancers impersonate, because something that may look like a fish to an outsider is a man to the villagers. The masks are seldom seen in collections outside the area because the villagers are vague as to their where-

abouts, and they are both large and fragile, making transport and display difficult. The Hamburg Museum in Germany, however, has a superb display.

The Kilenge people of western New Britain carve wooden masks similar to those of the Huon Gulf of New Guinea. These are danced at circumcision ceremonies. Much more spectacular are those called *bukumo*, which are danced at a later rite, when the boys have their ears pierced and their hair cut. The base is a carved and painted oval wooden mask, which is surrounded by cut leaves of palm and long canes, each of the latter with a feather inserted at the tip. This creates a disc some 12ft (3.6m) across, which ripples and sways to striking effect when danced.

About 20 miles (30km) east of New Britain is New Ireland. In the north-western part of this island considerable quantities of the mask known as *tatanua* are made for performances related to the *Malanggan*, a second burial ceremony that not only commemorates the deceased but also introduces new initiates. It is a major event, involving a complex marshalling of resources. After the death of a chief the clan have to

New Ireland, wood and fibre
Larger and more elaborate than the tatanua *masks,* kepong *masks such as this (**above**) were used in* Malanggan *ceremonies to mark the second burial of a deceased. They are rarer than the* tatanua.

New Ireland, wood, fibre, cloth, shell and metal
Tatanua *masks from New Ireland (**left**) are distinguished by the tall fibre median crest, often whitened with chalk. Occasionally the mask may have a small dance ornament inserted in the mouth.*

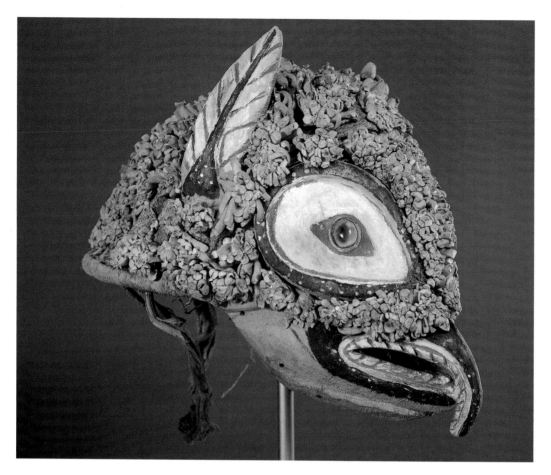

New Ireland, wood, shell, fibre, sponge, late nineteenth century This mask (left) representing an owl is a particularly naturalistic example. The opercula of the turbo petholatus *shell with its green spot on a white ground adds a particularly realistic touch.*

Pentecost Island, Vanuatu, wood This mask (right) is without doubt one of the finest to have survived from Melanesia. Height: 13½in (34.5cm) Sotheby's London 1978, £180,000

have the time to gather the necessary number of pigs and grow the yams for a series of feasts marking the building of the *Malanggan* house. The celebrations range from minor feasts marking the cutting of the trees for the carvings, to the final festival when the house is completed and the initiates are ready to emerge from their seclusion. The *tatanua* represent deceased persons and each in fact is given the name of a dead man. They are not abandoned in the *Malanggan* house after the performance, but are instead saved for the next. The masks have wooden faces, carved with square jaws and coloured red, black and white on the natural wooden ground—a decorative scheme used also for the house. To this wooden face is attached a high curved headdress of cane, covered in fibres, bark or trade cloth, encrusted with white chalk, and inset with sticks, seeds or twisted fibres; any or all of these are used in a variety of ways as panels, with cursive borders each side of a high median crest of brown fibres, resembling the helmet crest of a Roman centurion. The eyes are made from snail shells, which can give the masks a ferocious expression.

Other masks have broader faces than the *tatanua,* are carved in wood, and also have inset shell eyes, but the headdress is usually of tufted fibres; large wooden ears are inserted on each side and a wooden carving is thrust into the mouth, sometimes a stuffed hornbill head. Some masks can have exotic crests made from wooden insertions, and others, rarely, are carved as

pig heads. The exact function of these masks varies and it is usually impossible to discover them once they are removed from their context.

About 1,000 miles (1,600km) south-east of New Guinea lies the group of islands called Vanuatu (formerly New Hebrides). Society on the islands is carefully graded, and on one of the largest islands—Malekula—the rituals, regalia and titles associated with the levels of social prestige have been studied in detail. The different croton leaves each grade is allowed to wear, for example, are carefully specified. The masks in southern Malekula are linked to the death of chiefs and the circumcision of youths. Structures are erected in a compound *(longhor)* and feasts are given at intervals to mark the progress. The masks and headdresses are known as *temes mbalmbal (temes* being spirit) and are made of perishable materials that are abandoned after the ceremony. The mask is usually of conical form—typically a section of bamboo, split into strips, splayed and joined at the top; the free ends are fastened into a ring of mangrove wood, and over this a mulch of vegetable material is laid. This is then painted in coloured pigments with motifs resembling a human face. Others are covered with spiders' web and are worn by men of high rank. The masks are made by the older men—it seems to be considered presumptious for a young man to make one. The lower grades wear headdresses without masks. Some masks are like tall tapered hats that sit on the dancer's shoulders, so he has to be led by

another dancer who walks before him wearing a trail of croton leaves. On the nearby island of Ambryn are made gaily painted headdresses resembling plumed cocked hats and also rare wooden masks with trailing fibre surrounds.

Another island in the Vanuatu group is Pentecost, where a wooden mask is worn, carved with a rather long, oval, face, domed forehead and strongly curved nose, the whole blackened with soot and oil. These masks are only rarely found in collections today and some fakes have been made in the 1980s. They bear a resemblance to the only carved masks found further south, on the island of New Caledonia. These masks do not represent the horde of ancestors, however, but a specific mythical being, Pijeva, who leads the dance of the dead in the country underwater. He wears a wooden face mask above a costume of net and black feathers. New Caledonian masks are often collected with the costume of attached black feathers, which vary greatly in length; sometimes they come to just below the shoulders and sometimes they cover the whole torso of the masquerader. The masks of Pentecost, however, never seem to be collected with the costume attached.

Vanuatu, fibre
*Vegetable fibre is the material most often used for masks from the various islands of Vanuatu, and they are usually painted in bright colours; in this example (**left**) the colours may have worn off.*

New Ireland, wood, fibre, late nineteenth century
*A fine and unusual mask from New Ireland (**right**), this was collected at the end of the last century.*
Height: 10¼in (26cm)

ASIAN MASKS

The diversity of Asian cultures, religions and geography is borne out by the startling variety of masks illustrated in this chapter. These range from the fantastical intricacies of multi-coloured Gurula *bird masks from Sri Lanka to the stylized simplicity of white Noh masks from Japan.*

Asia is by far the largest and most populous continent in the world, so it is not surprising that it has a great variety and abundance of masks. Few societies have been entirely without them. However, as this book concentrates on masks that are available to collectors, it discusses only the following areas of production, mainly in south-east and east Asia: Indonesia; Sri Lanka; India and neighbouring countries; and finally Japan.

INDONESIA: SUMATRA AND BORNEO
The Republic of Indonesia consists of more than 13,000 islands (about half of which are inhabited) lying between the Indian and Pacific oceans. The islands stretch for more than 3,000 miles (4,800km) from the northern tip of Sumatra to Irian Jaya in the east, encompassing considerable climatic, geographical and cultural differences. Irian Jaya (the western part of New Guinea) is politically part of Indonesia, but culturally it belongs with Melanesia, and so is discussed in the Oceanic section of this book. Sumatra, Borneo and Java are the largest islands of Indonesia, and Bali—although small—is one of the most famous and beautiful.

Sumatra, the easternmost island of Indonesia, stretches some 1,200 miles (1,900km) from north to south across the equator. In the north of the island the Batak live in the area around Lake Toba, which gives its name to what is probably the oldest of the main groups who make up the Batak: the Toba, Karo, Pakpak, Simalungun, Angkola and Mandailing. The Toba live on Samosir island in the middle of the lake and on the shores to the west and south. The Batak were well known among their neighbours for their ferocity. Members of the community who violated religious laws might be eaten, and drinking the blood of a sacrificed prisoner of war was thought to be a way of strengthening one's *tondi* or soul.

The village is the principal political unit and is headed by a chief who is responsible for the most important religious ceremonies and for offerings to the ancestor spirits. Witchcraft was practised by the *datu*, or sorcerer, though in some instances this role might also be performed by the chief. The *datu* kept recipes for various powerful concoctions in a book of

Sri Lanka, wood
Sanni *masks were used to exorcise the spirits which cause disease. Each mask represents an ailment or deformity; this one* (**above left**) *may be deafness.*
Height: 7¾in (18.5cm)

Thailand, papier mâché
This mask would have been used in Khon *plays, which feature characters taken from the great Indian epics such as the* Ramayana.
Height: 22¼in (56.5cm)

folded bark, called *pustaka*. One such medicine, *puk-puk*, was used to activate the long staffs carved with figures used by the *datu*. It was made from a human heart or brain, usually that of a child kidnapped from an enemy village and forced to drink molten lead.

The most familiar mask of the Batak is that of the *sina*, a mythical beast whose head, carved with a tall crest and usually incised with scrolls, adorns houses, sarcophagi and the majority of small ritual objects. These masks were not carved to be worn, but masks were worn in ceremonies connected with the death of important men of a village. Masked dancers, accompanied by music, followed the coffin to the tomb. One such mask consists of a hornbill head attached to the top of a rattan frame, the dancer's head and body being covered with cloth. Costumes known as *hoda-hoda* were also worn and represent horses with naturalistically carved wooden heads. This tradition almost certainly derives from India, as must the similar dance with a two-dimensional horse popular today in Java. In former times the wearers of these masks were said to be sacrificed when they reached the place of burial, so that their spirits might accompany the deceased on his voyage to the next world. One or more slaves might also be sacrificed at the same time.

Among the Karo Batak, large masks of human form were worn by sorcerers at funerals. These are of helmet form, with pierced eyes and mouths and darkened faces. The mouths often have a broad grin, with carved teeth. On some fine and early examples, copper is applied to the forehead and nose and about the eyes and mouth, and horsehair is attached to the top of the head. The masked dancer would also hold a pair of wooden hands. Among the Simalungun Batak, the masks worn in funerary ceremonies are smaller and painted white, with embellishments in red and black. Goat- or horsehair is sometimes attached about the border and may also form a moustache or beard. Among the Toba Batak the human masks were placed in miniature houses built on the tomb, whereas among the Karo they were retained by the *datu* for use at ceremonies in the future.

Borneo is the third largest island in the world (after Greenland and New Guinea), but is thinly populated. Only the southern two thirds are under the political jurisdiction of Indonesia, the northern parts being made up of Sabah and Sarawak (both part of Malaysia) and the Sultanate of Brunei. The Dayaks are the longest-established inhabitants of the island and live inland in the rain forests, while more recent immigrants have settled along the coasts. The name Dayak actually means 'inlander' or 'uplander' and is generally used by writers today, and indeed by the Dayak themselves, to cover many different groups. Despite differences such as language and art, they have many similarities in their economic and religious life. For most Dayak groups, rice is the staple crop and many of their ceremonies are connected with the rice-growing season.

For the mask collector the Kayan and Kenyah related groups are perhaps the most notable. Highly distinctive masks, called *hudo*, are used during a dance feast held shortly after sowing time, to protect the young rice plants from evil influences (such as rodents) and to propitiate the rice spirits. These masks may represent humans or animals, including wild boar, birds, monkeys and crocodiles. The masks have bulging eyes and large ears resembling the wings of a butterfly. Ear ornaments are often suspended and horns inserted at the tip. Noses or beaks are usually long and pointed and the prominent mouth or snout is carved with teeth, sometimes large fangs. On some examples the lower jaw is articulated to be opened and closed by the wearer. When danced, the mask is surmounted by a woven rattan dome into which hornbill feathers are inserted, but this is usually missing in specimens brought back to the west. Painted bands, spots, and scrolls in red, white and black cover the entire surface. The scroll is a motif that occurs on

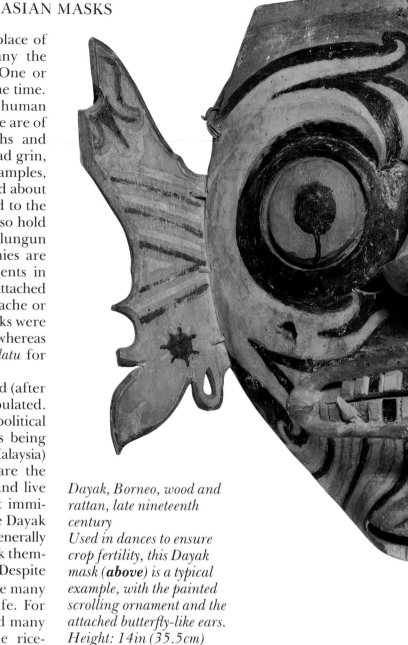

Dayak, Borneo, wood and rattan, late nineteenth century
*Used in dances to ensure crop fertility, this Dayak mask (**above**) is a typical example, with the painted scrolling ornament and the attached butterfly-like ears.*
Height: 14in (35.5cm)

almost all Kenyah and Kayan Dayak artefacts and is associated with the *aso*, usually described by writers as a mythical dog or dragon. Three other types of mask are typical among the Dayak of Long Segar in East Kalimantan. *Kitaq* are large painted masks of human form, with long elegant scrolls to each side; *hudoq taing* is a large wild boar mask; and *hudoq kibah* are hood masks, the faces being made of a panel of coloured beadwork with typical scrolling designs and with three copper caps in place of the eyes and mouth. They are worn by women, who sway their heads from side to side and move slowly.

Masks are used by the Dayak tribes of Sarawak in northern Borneo on various occasions. Those used in ceremonies connected with the harvest are less frightening and grotesque than those intended to represent demons. The masks from this area have smaller features than the *hudo* masks, nose and ears being of more naturalistic size. The surface is coloured with lime and soot, and hair, beards and moustaches

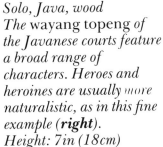

Solo, Java, wood
The wayang topeng *of*
the Javanese courts feature
a broad range of
characters. Heroes and
heroines are usually more
naturalistic, as in this fine
*example (**right**).*
Height: 7in (18cm)

are sometimes applied with monkey- or horsehair or strands of sugar palm.

In southern Borneo, grotesque masks are worn by clowns in funeral ceremonies, called *tiwah*. Behind the masks the clowns have licence to perform various pranks. The masks have bulging eyes, long noses and large ears and the open mouths are carved with teeth and long fangs. They are painted white with embellishments in black and red.

BALI AND JAVA

The appearance and function of masks from Bali and Java are quite different from those of tribal peoples of Sumatra and Borneo and show strong influences from India. In Java, troups of professional actors attached to the court performed masked dance dramas, the stories being most frequently based on the great Indian epics the *Ramayana* and the *Mahabharata*. This form of dance theatre, called *wayang topeng*, almost certainly developed from the puppet theatre, which is known to have existed as early as the eleventh century. The earliest type, *wayang kulit*, were shadow puppets made of perforated leather (*wayang* literally means 'shadow', and *kulit* 'leather'). Later forms were *wayang klitik*, flat wooden puppets, and *wayang golek*, three-dimensional puppets manipulated with rods. In the *wayang topeng*, dancers imitate the movements and speech of the puppets. A performance might contain 30 or even more masks representing different characters. The masks are small and light and are painted in various colours, which help to identify the character represented. Noble characters are refined in appearance, and vulgar ones are grotesque, with exaggerated features. Minor characters speak in the performance, but major ones do not, their lines being spoken by the *dalang* or producer. As long ago as the sixteenth century, however, the *wayang topeng* declined in popularity and was superseded by the *wayang orang*, in which the dancers are unmasked.

Tibet
This is one of several types of demonic masks worn in mystery plays called tsham *which were performed in Buddhist monasteries. The plays sometimes involved large numbers of characters and were therefore very costly to produce.*

One of the most popular masked dances in Bali features a battle between Barong and Rangda, symbolizing the struggle between good and evil. Barong personifies good, but is also a mischievous creature. In one of the most dramatic moments in the dance, Rangda, the evil witch, puts the supporters of Barong into a trance in which they try to stab themselves with their swords. Barong, with equally effective magic, prevents the weapons from harming them and they rush around madly attempting to stab themselves. Finally, good triumphs over evil. Both masks are fantastic and brightly painted with bulging eyes. Barong usually takes the form of a dragon, tiger, cow or boar, and Rangda usually has large fangs and a long, lolling tongue. Both have elaborate costumes to complement the masks; Rangda also has long nails with which she claws the air.

The Balinese *topeng* are chronicle plays of a more secular nature, dealing with amorous adventures, heroic deeds and court intrigues, in the lives of kings, noblemen and warriors. Actors wear small masks similar in style to the *wayang topeng* masks of Java.

SRI LANKA

The importance of the masking traditions of Sri Lanka (formerly Ceylon) is clearly indicated by the large number of fine examples to be found in western collections and museums today. Apart from masks used in processions and festivals, Sri Lanka is notable for two distinct groups of masks: those used in curative rituals called *tovil*; and those used in dance-dramas, such as the *kolam*. All are made of a light wood, usually kadura, which has to be seasoned for several weeks before it is carved.

The *sanni yakuma* is a night-long ceremony in which dancers wear *sanni* masks representing demon spirits responsible for causing disease. The ceremony is intended to exorcise the evil spirit responsible for a particular disease and thus restore the sufferer to health. Probably the most striking and certainly one of the largest of all south-east Asian masks is the *maha-kola-sanni-yaka*, the lord of the *sanni* masks. The large figure stands on a mask, holding the bodies of one or more victims in his hands and sometimes with another in the fangs of his large mouth. On each side is a panel of nine smaller masks, his assistants, each responsible for a particular disease or deformity, such as blindness, hallucinations, dumbness, rheumatism and boils. The group is flanked by cobras and further cobras issue from the top of the main mask's head. The quality of the carving and painting on old examples is extremely fine.

Kolam masks are of a more secular nature and are worn in ceremonial dance-dramas, especially in the southern and western coastal areas. There are more than 100 different characters, many having counterparts in the Indian folk masking tradition, from which they must have derived. These include *Gurula*, the local equivalent of Garuda, the mythical bird on which the Hindu god Vishnu rode. Among the various animal masks is the tiger (although the animal itself is not found in Sri Lanka). One of the most frequently encountered of *kolam* masks is the snake demon, *naga rassa*. This has large bulging eyes and wide-open mouth with painted teeth. The headdress is a large cobra and the separately carved ears are coiled cobras.

Kolam natima is said to have originated in the craving of a pregnant Indian queen to see a new kind of masked dance. While her despairing husband slept, Sara or Sakka (the local equivalent of the Hindu god Indra) arranged for masks to be carved. They were placed in the royal gardens, together with the book of the play, and the following morning they were discovered by a terrified gardener. The queen was delighted with the performance that followed.

Although there have been many changes in performance practice over the years, the play generally opens with a herald recounting the story of the pregnant queen. The herald introduces a pair of warriors (or sometimes a warrior and his wife), who enact a rumbustious scene. This always seems to have been a highly popular part of the performance, for warrior masks are among the most common and are found in many collections. The warriors are followed by a variety of human characters (government official, village headman, money-lender and so on), each wearing a small but distinctive face mask that reveals his identity. The king and queen wear the largest and tallest masks of all; they are so top-heavy that they have to move slowly to their seats, where they take no active part in the performance. There are also various animals and demons.

INDIA, THAILAND, TIBET AND NEPAL

The art of India has been an inspiration to Sri Lanka and many other neighbouring countries, but masks have played a comparatively small role in Indian culture and examples are fairly uncommon in western collections and museums. They are found mainly in folk traditions, rather than directly in the service of the great religions. The *Chau* dance festival of Bihar in northern India, for example, has close similarities to the *kolam* dramas of Sri Lanka. It is held in the spring in honour of Nata Bhairaba, an aspect of Shiva (or Siva), the Hindu god who was Lord of the Dance. The themes may be secular, religious or mythical, but all symbolize the victory of good over evil. The masks used were originally made of wood but today they are usually of papier mâché.

Masks produced by tribal groups in India are usually simple and dramatic, having more in common with the masks of Africa than those of the rest of India. Those made by the Bhuiyas of Orissa in northeast India, for example, are intended for divination before the annual hunt, while those made by the Khonds (or Konds), who live in the same state, are connected with their former practice of human sacrifice. The masks of the Muria of the Madhya Pradesh region of central India are worn by young boys acting out short themes from daily life, while the Gonds, who also live in Madhya Pradesh and neighbouring provinces, wear masks for dancing during weddings.

Indian influence on the art of far-eastern countries spread with Buddhism and Hinduism. In Thailand, theatrical performances include themes from the great Indian epics such as the *Ramayana*. The masks often have tall elaborate gilt headdresses. In Tibet, Lamaism (a form of Buddhism) uses masks in mystery plays, *tsham*, held in the monasteries. These may have developed from ancient fertility exorcism rites, and themes include the Dance of a Hundred Gods (performed only in the largest monasteries in view of the cost of the masks and costumes), which recounts the birth of the Buddha and the introduction of Buddhism into Tibet. Out of context, and stripped of the attributes worn or held by the characters, these masks are often difficult to identify.

The mask of death is a type frequently encountered in the Buddhist temples of Tibet; it is not a result of a morbid fascination with death, but rather a celebration of the victory of religious teaching over death. The masks, carved as a human skull, often have a crown of smaller skulls at the top. Masks representing deities frequently have ferocious expressions and wide-open mouths with long teeth. Crowns of small skulls are common as is the 'third eye' at the centre of the forehead. A wide variety of material is used, including papier mâché, wood and hide.

In Nepal a number of tribal groups such as the Magar and Gurung used masks that have a thick black crusty patina; this results from the accumulation of

years of smoke from storage in the rafters of houses. Many are of simple and striking form, with rough, vigorous carving. Eyes and mouths are often simple circles or rectangles. Fur is frequently applied as hair, beard or moustache. Many tribal masking traditions have been gradually replaced by the spread of Hinduism and Buddhism.

JAPAN

Japan has a rich tradition of theatrical masks. They belong to three groups, the Gigaku, Bugaku and Noh (or No), which developed in that chronological order. They are made from lacquer and wood and are always painted, as much time being spent on decoration as on modelling. The *men-uchi* (carvers) were limited in the way they carved a particular mask type by *honmen* (the traditional prototype of a mask), and any deviation from this was considered an artistic failure. The use of colour also followed strict rules and was significant in identifying a character. More freedom could, however, be exercised when making masks representing demons and mythical creatures.

The earliest type of theatrical mask known in Japan is Gigaku ('skilled music'), said to have been introduced from China by a Korean migrant named Mimashi. Artists from Iran, Tibet, Manchuria, Korea, Indochina and Indonesia performed at the court of the T'ang dynasty (AD 618–906), and these diverse racial types were represented by Gigaku masks carved in a naturalistic style usually depicting a fixed emotion or state such as anger or drunkenness. Gigaku performances were comic or coarse skits, played among crowds near Buddhist temples or in open squares and accompanied by an orchestra of three main instruments: flute, drum and gong. Only 15 or so characters featured in Gigaku performances, including *Baramon*, an Indian Brahmin, *Kongo Rikishi*, protector of Buddhism (*rikishi* meaning 'mighty one' and *kongo* 'thunderbolt' or 'diamond'), *Suiko-o* and *Suiko-ju*, drunken revellers (either Central Asian or Iranian), *Taikofu*, a feeble tottering old man, and *Shishi*, the lion.

Gigaku waned in popularity in the ninth century and was superseded by Bugaku. Bugaku also featured a variety of racial types, but the masks have more stylized features and often ferocious expressions, though the dances were more subtle than those of Gigaku and used a more elaborate orchestra accompanied by singers. Performances were reserved for festivals, commemorations and religious ceremonies and were patronized by the Imperial court. Older masks covered all of the face and the back of the head, while later styles covered only the face. A characteristic of the Bugaku mask is the use of free-moving parts, which emphasize the rhythmn of the dance. The most elaborate of these articulated masks was *Genjoraku*, with movable eyes, nose, chin and cheeks.

Noh drama was an entirely Japanese invention, originating in about the fourteenth century, and it is still considered one of the purest and most distinctive expressions of the nation's culture. The masks are more subtle than earlier types, hiding only the face rather than the entire front of the head. Performances were originally mainly for the samurai class, with occasional benefit and gala shows for ordinary people. Noh drama is poetic, stylized, musical and extremely slow, its solemnity recalling a religious ceremony.

The principal actors wore magnificent heavily brocaded robes; masks therefore had to be bold to be in keeping with them, yet suble enough to convey the sensitive emotions required of the performers. They were made of light kiriri wood and painted with distemper, with a thin layer of lacquer on the inside. Human characters gradually developed into standard types, such as 'young woman' or 'old man'. Certain characteristics, such as a small variation in the arrangement of hair, enabled these to be divided into particular types favoured for individual roles. Ghosts, demons, spirits and gods also feature. All parts were played by men or boys. Those representing females, gods and demons were necessarily masked, but some male roles were performed without masks.

The finest Noh masks are among the most beautiful produced anywhere in the world, combining subtle stylization with delicate naturalism. Among the most popular and familiar is the 'young woman', representing the traditional Japanese ideal of beauty. She is depicted with long straight black hair parted in the centre, with carefully arranged strands framing the forehead. The face is whitened, with the eyebrows painted in black high on the forehead. Lips are reddened and teeth painted black. Masks representing old men have carefully painted or carved wrinkles; hair is often attached through holes carved at the top of the head and also for beard and moustache. Certain masks were used to represent one specific character who occurs in just one particular play. One such character is *Shojo* ('the Dancing Orang-utan'), a drunken youth, characterized by his red face, a result of too much sake. His lips are parted in a half-smile, the upper and lower teeth exposed, and he has a tousled fringe and dimples. The mask is small and earless and always worn with a long red wig.

Kyogen plays were performed as comic interludes during a Noh drama and were in stark contrast to the elegance of the main work. Colloquial language was used and fewer characters wore masks, which were much less subtle than Noh masks.

Unlike maskmakers from most parts of the world, some of the Japanese carvers signed their work and won renown for their skill. The Deme or Demme family, who flourished particularly in the seventeenth century, were perhaps the best known. Like other mask carvers, they supplemented their income by carving miniature masks as *netsuke*—small toggles used to attach various small pouches and containers to the belt of the traditional Japanese costume.

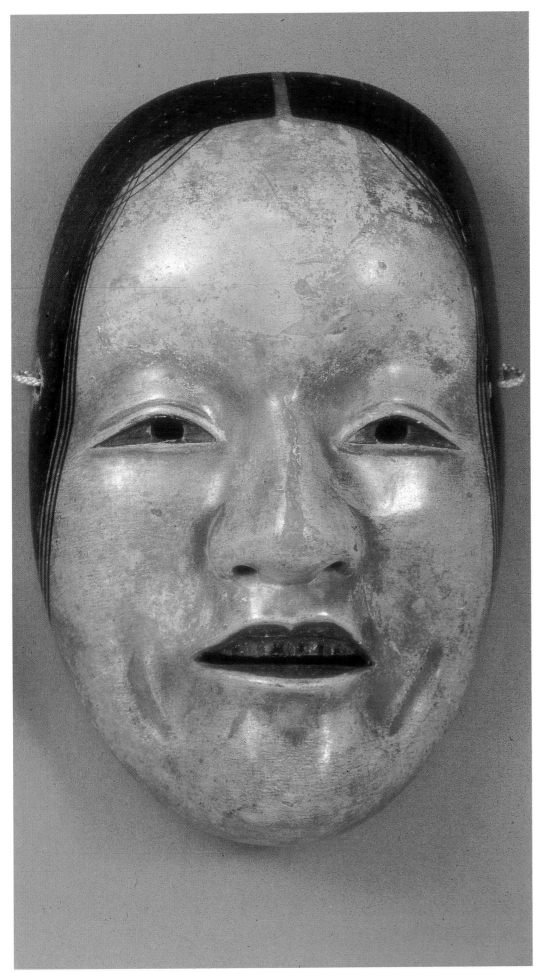

Japan, wood, nineteenth century
*This mask (**left**), used in the Noh plays, represents the ideal of a beautiful woman, Ko-Omote.*
Height: 8½in (21.6cm)

Japan, wood, eighteenth century
*Kyogen plays were performed as comic interludes to the Noh plays, and this mask (**above**) is in stark contrast to the one on the left. It represents a woman, Oto (also known as Okame), the most popular of Kyogen characters.*
Height: 7⅝in (19.5cm)
Christie's London 1988, £1500

NEW WORLD MASKS

Masks from the Americas comprise an enormous range of styles. They are no less linked to ritual and superstition than are masks from Africa or Asia, and some, such as the famous transformation masks of the Kwakiutl, are among the most dazzling and sophisticated examples of tribal art from anywhere in the world.

The masking tradition in the Americas dates back very many centuries. Archaeological finds among the ruins of the ancient civilizations of South and Central America give some indication of the significance of masks in these societies. In North America, too, the tradition can be traced back to long before the first European contact in the sixteenth century.

NORTH AMERICA

Wooden masks from as early as AD 800 were found at the end of the nineteenth century on the west coast of Florida, and stone and clay funerary masks have been found in ancient sites in the southern Great Lakes area. Since the sixteenth century, four areas have been notable for mask production: the north-west coast, the east, the south-west and the Arctic.

THE NORTH-WEST

The masks of the north-west coast are carved in a large variety of shapes and forms and painted in startling colours. The principal tribes in the area, the Tlingit, Tsimshian, Haida, Bella Bella, Bella Coola, Kwakiutl and Nootka, live along the 1,000-mile (1,600km) stretch of coastline from the Columbia River in Washington State to Yakutat Bay in Alaska. This is a rocky coastline of endless bays and inlets with a multitude of small islands; wooded slopes come down to stony shores, appearing and disappearing through the mists that usually shroud the coast. A skein of larger islands lies parallel to the coast. The rainfall in the area is the highest in the world, but warm currents mean an ice-free zone far further north and for a much longer time than for the same latitude on the east coast. Although they speak different languages, the tribes of the region share a common culture and masks made in widely separated communities may share distinctive characteristics, such as

Tlingit, wood, mid-nineteenth century
*This shaman's mask (**above left**) is essentially human; it has bear-like ears, however, and a pierced mouth.*
Height: 10⅝in (27cm)

Tlingit, wood, fibre and feathers
*This mask (**right**) has a headband inset with feathers and hair; others might have been decorated with inset seal whiskers or plaited cedar bark.*
Height: 11in (28cm) Christie's London 1976, £16,000

asymmetrical painted designs representing the stylized features of spirits. However, as a generalization, the masks from the northern groups tend to be smaller and more naturalistic, while those of the southern tribes tend to be larger, very fantastical and brightly coloured, with a predominance of red, white and blue.

Among the naturalistic masks from the north, most notably those of the Haida, many seem to be portraits and are carved with such features as moustaches, wrinkles and pierced ears. Some are shown wearing oval lip-plugs, to represent women of high rank; others, notably from the third quarter of the nineteenth century, are clearly intended to represent Europeans, with the fashionable hairstyles and beards of the time. Many of the masks have elaborate contraptions to open and close the eyes and mouth, and among the southern tribes such sophistication was taken to extremes in the transformation masks of the Kwakiutl. In these a mask opens to reveal yet another mask inside, transforming the dancer into another spirit.

Many North American Indians lead a nomadic existence, following herds of buffalo across the plains, but the tribes of the north-west coast spend most of their time fishing. They preserve their abundant catch by smoking, drying and processing for oil, providing food for the long winter days. As a result, there is little subsistence work to be done during the winter months, which can therefore be devoted to leisure activities. This has led to the development of a sophisticated ceremonial tradition centred around the famous potlach feasts. These occasions were used by the host to assert his social status and involved lavish hospitality and festivities, including dancing.

Tribes were divided into clans and moieties (literally 'halves') named after a real or mythological ancestor. Tlingit society, for example, was divided into two moieties, the Raven and the Eagle (or further south the Wolf). Each clan owned a number of animal crests, personal names, songs and dances. A great variety of animals, fish and birds were adopted as crests. Those not playing an important part in the economy were more common; among the Tlingit they included the raven, hawk, brown bear, killer whale, otter, mouse, frog, and even wood-worm. The right to wear such crests, and ancestral rights to dances, territories and other privileges, were witnessed when a chief held a potlach and distributed these valuables to his heirs and friends.

Among the Kwakiutl in the south, the winter season of ceremonies was known as *Tsetseka*, and the principal dance, the *Hamatsa*, formed part of a ritual that lasted for at least four days. Initiates possessed by the spirit Bakbakwalanooksiwae (Cannibal-at-the-North-End-of-the-World) were inspired with the desire to eat human flesh. They were abducted and taken into the woods, where they were taught the ways of the group and were later returned to the village as fully-fledged members of the society. In their absence, dancers rep-

Kwakiutl, wood and feathers
Kwakiutl masks are the most dramatic and largest of the Northwest coast masks. In this transformation mask the mythical raven opens to reveal one of its descendents of human form.

resenting mythical creatures associated with this spirit appeared from behind painted screens and danced about an open fire. When Dzoonokwa, the terrifying giant of Kwakiutl mythology, leapt from behind the screen making a fearsome sound, a chill would go through the audience.

Other masks are the Thunderbird, who caused thunder by the beat of his wings, and bird monsters who lived on human flesh. The spectacular bird monster masks measured up to 8ft (2.4m) in length and it would have required considerable strength and skill to operate the pulleys that caused the beaks to snap shut in time to the songs accompanying the dances. Other dancers included the fool dancer, Noolmhal, whose tasks included keeping the spec-

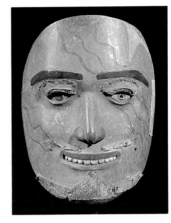

Tongass, Southern Tlingit, wood
*The eyelids on this mask (**above**) could be articulated by the wearer pulling a short stick.*
Length: 9in (23cm)
Christie's London 1976, £36,000

Tongass, Southern Tlingit, wood and hide
*This mask (**below**) has an articulated jaw. Along with the example above it was collected by W. E. Gordon, R.N., in 1851–4.*
Height: 10in (25.5cm)
Christie's London 1976, £20,000

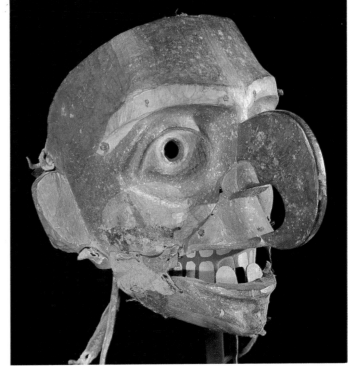

tators under control and possibly supplying human flesh for the bird monsters. It is not known whether actual cannibalism at one time formed part of these rituals; certainly by the end of the nineteenth century it was no longer practised.

The Rockies to the east of the coastal region are too snow-bound in winter to support permanent settlement and the tribes of the Great Plains do not wear masks, although some have elaborate headdresses. It is on the other side of the Great Lakes that masquerading communities are once more encountered.

THE EAST

The masks of the False Face Society were first recorded in 1687, when the first Europeans visited the lower Great Lakes area, but there is no evidence to indicate how long the society had existed before then. The society was at that time, and still is, found among the five main tribes of the Iroquois nation: the Mohawk, Oneida, Onandaga, Cayuga and Seneca. Its main purpose was the prevention and cure of diseases, achieved through both public and private ceremonies. An Iroquois legend tells of the contest between the Creator of the World and the first False Face spirit to decide who should rule the world. The Creator agreed to acknowledge the superiority of the False Face if he could command a mountain to come to them. The False Face shook his rattle and commanded the mountain, but it came only part of the way. The Creator then summoned the mountain; it approached from behind False Face, who turned around impatiently just as the mountain came near, striking him in the face. It broke his nose and caused him to twist his mouth in pain. In consequence of losing the contest, False Face was charged by the Creator with the task of driving out disease from the earth. The first False Face, also known as the Great Doctor, then gave the power of healing the sick to humans if they agreed to carve masks ('false faces') in his image and make offerings to him of tobacco and corn mush.

Masks representing the Great Doctor are fairly easy to distinguish and occur among all five main tribes of the Iroquois nation. There are several other lesser spirits, that are more difficult to identify, notably the Common Faces. These are beings thought to live in the forests; they are sometimes described as being deformed, with crippled legs or hunched backs, or even as having no bodies or limbs but only faces.

A person might decide to join the False Face Society to find a cure for an illness or after a dream of impending sickness. The candidate would then be expected to give a feast (and would thereafter be required to do so annually) and would need to acquire a mask. He could inherit one, could carve it himself, commission someone to carve it for him or borrow one, and his dream might indicate which of these options he was to adopt. The mask might then be carved to represent the image in his dream or it might be interpreted for him by a seer and then carved. Such a system led to a considerable diversity in appearance and makes the identification and interpretation of some masks very difficult.

To carve a mask, a tree (usually basswood) was selected in the forest and offerings of tobacco were lit at the base. The mask was roughed out while still on the tree and the block would then be removed and taken home by the carver to be finished at leisure. Today, masks might be simply carved from an available block of wood, but in earlier times it was considered important to remove the block of wood from the tree without causing the tree to die; it was no doubt thought that the continued existence of the tree added to the potency of the mask. The mask was painted red if work on the carving began in the morning and black if carving began in the afternoon. This symbolism refers to the belief that the Great Doctor lives on the rim of the world and follows the path of the sun. Horsehair was attached and metal rings have frequently been applied about the eyes, perhaps to enhance the effect of the mask when danced around a fire. The initiate and his mask would then take part in the ceremony, in which prayers were recited and offerings of tobacco were burned. Tiny bags of tobacco were also hung from the mask and the mask was then invested with the power to cure.

Public ceremonies were held in the spring and autumn to wipe out disease in the community. Members of the society, wearing masks and carrying turtle-shell rattles, would visit each house in turn, shouting and chasing out disease. After this they would proceed to the longhouse, where they banged their rattles on the door and crawled in towards a fire in the centre. After speeches honouring the spirits and offerings of tobacco, the sick came forward and were treated with ashes blown onto their heads and rubbed into their hair. Payment was made in the form of tobacco and corn mush. For a similar payment a private treatment could be made at a patient's house. Only certain ailments could be cured, however: those of the head, shoulders and joints. False Faces are particularly concerned with nosebleed, earache, toothache, sore eyes, facial paralysis and facial swelling. They were sometimes assisted in these rituals by an associated society known as the Husk Faces, believed to be a more recent development. Members wore masks, slightly smaller than those of the False Face Society, made of coils of braided or twined husks. They were made by women but worn only by men. Miniature False Face masks were also made as charms for protection against sickness or witchcraft.

The False Face mask itself is considered an object of remarkable power and has to be treated with great care. Offerings of tobacco must be made regularly and the mask must be stored face down, with the rattle placed in the hollow at the back, together with a package of tobacco. According to the Seneca, an upward facing mask is a sign of disrespect and is associated with death. If hung on a wall for storage, a mask must either face the wall or remain covered. On the death of the owner, a mask might be buried with the owner, given to another member of the society, or sold. If sold, an offering of tobacco is made and the mask is told it is leaving and is instructed not to cause harm either to the new owner or to the old one. There are tales of masks coming back to haunt their former owners, and Iroquois believe that a fire in the New York State Museum in 1911 was the result of the museum's failure to give tobacco to the masks while they were in their care.

THE SOUTH-WEST

The third principal area of mask production in North America is in the south-west, in the states of Arizona and New Mexico. The Indians of the Rio Grande area are known as Pueblos, a name also given to the permanent villages of mud buildings in which they live. They are farmers, dependent on crops of corn, beans and squash. For communities of farmers living in such an

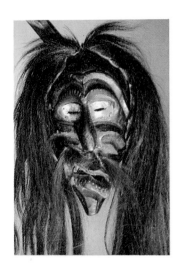

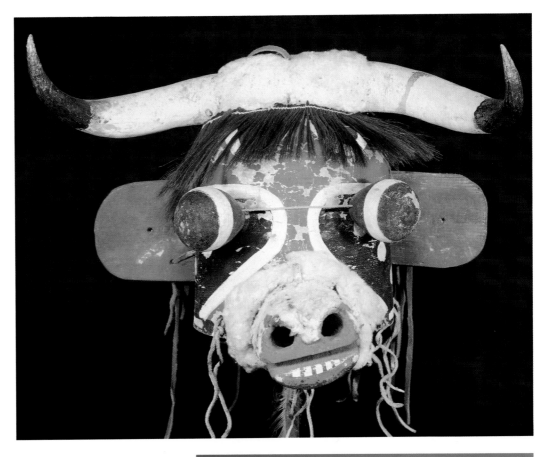

Iroquois, wood, metal and hair
The masks of the False Face Society are usually realistic: the extensive wrinkles on this example (**above**) are typical. The metal about the eyes would add to the dramatic effect when danced about a fire.

Pueblo, wood, hair, hide and horns
An unusual type of Pueblo mask, this bull (**above right**) is made of wood and is particularly naturalistic. Kachina masks were worn in ceremonies to mark various stages of the agricultural year.

Kwakiutl, wood, nineteenth century
Hamatsa *masks such as this (**right**) were used by the Kwakiutl during the winter season of ceremonies. Cords enable the wearer to move the eyes and beak.*
Length: 11½in (29cm)

arid climate, the main rituals are associated with water and crop fertility.

The Pueblo Indians believe that the natural phenomena of this world have a spiritual counterpart, or *kachina*, and the cult associated with these spirits encompasses the whole Pueblo community. The most familiar representation of *kachinas* are the wooden dolls that were traditionally carved by the men and given as gifts to children and women, particularly to girls of marriageable age. Dances form an important part of the rituals associated with the *kachina* cult; the masked dancers do not simply impersonate the *kachinas*, but embody them. Among the Hopi there are five major ceremonies during the *kachina* season, beginning with the winter solstice ceremony in December. The bean ceremony follows in February to mark the start of the growing season, which is also the time for initiation of children into the cult. At the end of February or the beginning of March is the Water

Serpent ceremony, and the cycle is completed at the close of the season by the Home Dance ceremony in July. It is so named because it is the last occasion on which the *kachinas* make their appearance before they return to what the Hopi believe to be their homes on the San Francisco peaks. Other ceremonies are held after July, but *kachina* dances do not form a part of the proceedings. Some ceremonies are held in secret in *kivas* or underground chambers, while others, including a number of one-day ceremonies, are held wholly or partly in public, in the plazas or village squares.

The masks worn by the dancers are constructed of hide. The most common type is composed of a cylinder made from two pieces of hide with a circular top. Ears, noses, snouts, horns and feather headdresses can then be attached to this base. Although the basic shape is simple, the vibrant painted decoration makes the Pueblo masks extremely striking. A simple painted motif, such as a hand or claw, may indicate

Inuit, Alaska, wood, cane
The masking tradition of
the Inuit may not date back
before the first European
*contact. This mask (**right**)*
is typical of examples from
Alaska, which are usually
small and often highly
elaborate with various
limbs and other items
about the border.
Height: 10¼in (26cm)

Iroquois, fibre, twentieth
century
Corn husk masks such as
*this (**above**) were worn by*
dancers who assisted the
False Faces. They were
probably a later
development.
Height: 13¾in (35cm)

the *kachina* represented, and the bold colours in which it is painted are symbolic. They are said to indicate the direction from which a *kachina* comes: yellow indicates north or north-west; blue or green, west or south-west; red, south or south-east; white, east or north-east; black indicates a downward direction. Because the basic construction of the masks was the same, a mask could be adapted for use on a subsequent occasion by adjustment of the appendages and by applying a further coat of paint. In addition to this most common type of mask, there are also half-masks, covering the upper part of the head with feathers and hair below, and circular masks.

THE ARCTIC

Sophisticated masking traditions exist among the Eskimos of the Arctic region, which stretches from the Bering Sea in the west to Greenland in the east, through Alaska and the islands of northern Canada. The climate in the north of this region is certainly inhospitable, but the Eskimos (or Inuit as they call themselves, preferring their term, meaning 'real people', to the derogatory 'Eskimo', meaning 'meat eaters') have adapted well to the environment. It provides an abundance of food, including seals, whales, walrus and various inland mammals (principally caribou), as well as fish. As on the north-west coast, the practice of

preserving food in the summer for the winter months has provided much leisure time in winter for the development of an artistic tradition. This finds its greatest expression in the extraordinary masks of the area. Ivory burial masks were made by the Eskimos perhaps as long as 2,000 years ago (some superb examples have been excavated), but their tradition of masks for dancing does not seem to be of great antiquity. Excavations at many pre-historic sites have yielded great numbers of wooden artefacts but have failed to unearth more than a few masks or fragments of masks. This may be in part because of the practice of destroying masks after a ritual, but as almost all the masks now in existence date from the nineteenth and twentieth centuries, it seems likely that the tradition developed, or expanded, after contact with Europeans.

Eskimo dancing masks were usually made by, or for, shamans, the men who provide the community's link with the spirit world. They were danced in winter ceremonies such as the Messenger Feast and Bladder Festival, intended to appease the spirits of the animals hunted for food and ensure continued success in the hunt. The masks represent spirits of the animals that play such an important role in the life of the Eskimo, and sometimes spirits associated with natural phenomena, such as the sun and the moon, or even spirits of places or ancient objects. They are not based on naturalistic physical appearance, but on images seen by the shaman on his visits to the spirit world. The mask would therefore inspire awe and wonder in the spectator at the ability of the shaman to communicate with another world, to which only he has access.

The most remarkable and fantastic of these masks are from the Bering Sea area. They are basically two-dimensional in form and almost all are painted, the most common colours being white, black, red and blue. Many are surrounded by willow bands that support a variety of appendages and pendants of wood, feathers and caribou fur. Composite masks also exist (though they are less elaborate than those of the northwest coast), an outer mask opening to reveal the soul of the animal spirit inside, or a human mask inside that of an animal, thus emphasizing the close link between the animal and human worlds. The dance was accompanied by singing and the beat of a drum and the lively movements of the masked male dancers contrasted with the graceful swaying of the women, who sometimes formed a chorus. The women also wore small finger masks—discs of wood with two holes to one side for the insertion of fingers, adorned with feathers and painted decoration.

SOUTH AMERICA

The dense rain forests of the Amazon are populated by a large number of different tribes. Travel in the area is difficult and dangerous, either overland or by boat, along the vast network of rivers and tributaries. Communications are consequently limited between the

Upper Xingu River, Brazil, wood, fibre, feathers, late nineteenth century
Masks from the area of the upper Xingu River are characterized by their rectangular form and the painted geometric decoration. Height: 25¼in (64cm)

various tribes, many of which, as a result, retain a highly distinctive artistic style. There is a vast array of different mask types, only a few of which can be mentioned here. The recent concern in the West about the plight of many of these peoples—in the wake of the destruction of their environment for cattle ranching and the search for minerals—has come too late to save many of them from extinction and one can only hazard an educated guess at the function of some of the masks they have left.

Among the Indians of the area of north-west Brazil and eastern Columbia—those of the Arawak and Tucano groups—large masks of barkcloth are made for use in mourning rites. After a death, all the deceased kinsmen are instructed by the headman to make a mask, and the elaborate preparations for the rites can take up to six months to complete. The masks are of conical form, coming down to the chest, with cylindrical projections for the arms and with a fibre fringe below. Eyeholes are not required, as the beaten fibrous material is sufficiently thin to allow the dancer to see through. The masks are painted with a variety of bold geometric designs in black and shades of brown; lozenges and triangles are particularly favoured, and facial features are sometimes painted. Tucano

EUROPEAN MASKS

Europe possesses a number of fascinating masquerade traditions performed in a variety of contexts. Some of them are influenced by cultures from other areas of the world, and many of the masquerades are pagan in origin; over the centuries, however, they have been accommodated within a broadly Christian framework.

Europe possesses a rich and varied mask-making heritage. Since Ancient Greece, professional actors have made use of masks, and in one of the continent's most famous theatrical traditions, the Italian *Commedia dell' arte*, masked performers played a central role. Masks are also found among peasant communities and are still worn to celebrate a wide range of festivals, many of which have ancient origins. The rural and urban masquerades did not invariably develop in isolation from one another and influences and counter-influences are readily detectable.

The earliest evidence of the use of masks in Europe comes from the cave of Trois Frères, in southern France, which is decorated with painted and 'engraved' images dating from about 15,000-8,000 BC. The cave walls are filled with overlapping depictions of bison, stags, reindeer, horses and ibex, in the midst of which are scattered human figures. These are thought to be ritual dancers, performing perhaps a sacred rite associated with hunting, and some are shown masked with animal heads. The most striking feature of the cave, however, is a painting, with engraved outlines, which shows a man wearing the head and antlers of a stag. Although the significance of this image remains unknown, archaeologists have speculated that it may represent a kind of powerful shaman or perhaps a supreme deity.

A direct link cannot be drawn between the rituals of Stone Age hunters in France and the customs of contemporary rural populations, but it is interesting that animal, or half-animal, characters still play an important part in numerous masquerades.

Horns and fur are worn by masked dancers in many European regions, and 'hairiness' has long been popularly associated with the non-human worlds of animals and spirits. Many of these folk festivals have pagan origins, although they have adopted Christian elements and have been incorporated into the Church's calendar.

Bavaria, Germany, wood, fibre, late eighteenth century
*Hairy characters are included in many European masquerades. This mask (**above left**) has long hair, bushy eyebrows and a flowing beard and moustache.*

Tyrol, Austria, painted wood, c. 1900
Noisy parades of masked characters are traditionally found in many Alpine regions. This Hutler *mask (**right**) has much in common with the masks worn during the* Schemenlaufen *festivals.*

BRITAIN

Some of the finest examples of animal masquerades are found in Britain. One of the best known of these is the 'horn dance' of Abbots Bromley in Stafford-shire, which traditionally takes place on the first or second Monday in September. Six dancers take part in the celebration, each one carrying a pair of antlers attached to a wooden deer's head mounted on a pole. They are accompanied by several other characters, including a simple hobby-horse with a small head and snapping jaws.

Although the British 'horn dance' is rare, the hobby-horse, of which there are several varieties, is quite widely distributed. Hobby-horses may be ac-companied by other performers, such as Morris dancers or, as used to be the case in Land's End in Cornwall, by 'guisers' masked and draped with bullock hides. The horse's head is often made from

Bavaria, Germany, painted wood
A pair of masks representing a man and a woman. The idealized couple have a sense of perfection lent to them by the wholly painted features. Such masks were also used in boisterous Schemenlaufen *festivals.*

inexpensive and readily available materials, and the carrier is usually concealed by a hanging cloth. In Bwca Lwyd in Wales the hobby-horse used to com-prise a painted canvas head stuffed with straw and mounted on a hay fork. Leather fastened to the prongs served as ears. A horse's skull set on top of a pole was used in some places, whereas in Thanet in Kent the head is traditionally carved from a single block of wood and is painted. By tugging on a leather lace, the carrier of the Kentish *hoden* horse can bang open and shut the hinged jaws.

Switzerland, painted wood, various materials, c. 1900
This festival mask was probably made in Basel. It is
distinguished by its elaborate headdress decorated with
ostrich feathers and artificial flowers.

Switzerland, painted wood, cloth, c. 1900
In Alpine regions, festivals are held in midwinter to
celebrate the victory of 'young' spring over 'old' winter.
This mask represents an old woman.

The Minehead hobby-horse in Somerset custom-arily appears between 30 April and 3 May. It has a fearsome tin mask, partly covered with a ribbon bon-net, which is hung from a boat-shaped frame. A hoop 6ft (1.8m) in diameter is used on the Padstow (Corn-wall) hobby-horse to support a long and fringed black tarpaulin. This May Day *Oss* has a small wooden head with snapping jaws and a fringe of hair. The letters O.B. appear on the conical hat worn by the horse and these are thought to represent either the initials of a long-dead resident of Padstow or an abbreviation of 'hobby-horse'.

The ghost-like *Mari Lwyd* of Glamorganshire and Carmarthenshire in Wales, a well-known Christmas visitor, contrasts markedly with other brightly colour-ed hobby-horses. Folklorists have likened the Welsh hobby-horse (*Y Mari Lwyd* probably means 'the grey mare') to the Irish horse of the feast of Samain. In parts of County Cork this ancient Celtic festival is traditionally marked by processions led by a white-robed man bearing the semblance of a horse's head. Samain, which is celebrated around 1 November, marks the end of the summer.

Aside from the hobby-horse, a variety of masked characters features in British folk festivals, especially those associated with the agricultural cycle. The Scot-tish *Bury Man* of West Lothian, who appears in August, wears a hat planted with 70 red roses and one red dahlia. His face is concealed by a back-to-front bala-clava hat, furnished with eyeholes, and is covered with sticky burrs from the burdock plant. A man cov-ered from head to foot in twisted straw braids tradi-tionally walks through the streets of Whitby (Yorkshire) on the Saturday before Plough Monday (the first Monday after the Christmas holidays). Straw charac-ters are also known in the Irish countryside, where young men, dressed in women's garments, used to wear cone-shaped festival masks made of straw.

AUSTRIA

Many other European peoples mark seasonal changes with celebrations involving masked performers. One of the best known of these masquerades takes place every three years, before the beginning of Lent, in the town of Imst in the Austrian Alps. Known as *Schemenlaufen* (*scheme* is an archaic word for 'mask' and *laufen* means 'to run'), this festival symbolizes the struggle between winter and spring for the domi-nation of nature. Only men may take part in this masquerade, which is held to frighten away the accumulated spirits and to ensure prosperity and a bountiful harvest in the coming year. The fearsome

masks and jangling bells worn by the participants, who follow a winding course through the town, are thought to put the evil demons to flight. The masks are carved in wood and the male ones can be distinguished by their beards, the female ones having smooth pink faces. Huge headdresses, decorated with braids and baubles, are also worn by the good characters. The runners are accompanied by witches, whose masks have goggle eyes and fang-like teeth. Their facial hair is made with either pigs' bristles or feathers. There is also a sorcerer, who wears a mask with a goatee beard and carries a magic sceptre, as well as a *Sackner* who throws handfuls of corn from his sack at the feet of the spectators. The onlookers may also be squirted with water from a syringe carried by a masked figure known as a *Spritzer*. The *Schemenlaufen* festival was once more widely distributed than it is today. For example, similar masked figures used to accompany the Nuremberg butchers' guild, a practice that was discontinued in 1539.

Rowdy processions are also held on Twelfth Night, which is associated with the pre-Christian deity Perchta, the custodian of the dead. According to German mythology, Perchta and her followers rush through the night, sometimes perpetrating good deeds, and sometimes bad. Their impersonators wear exotic horned and hairy masks, which are intended to frighten naughty children and to ensure the fertility of the crops. In Salzburg these masqueraders used to enact a ritual battle between the good characters, distinguished by their beautiful visages and ornate headdresses, and the evil ones, dressed in unkempt masks. Similar shaggy figures are known throughout the Bavarian, Swiss and Austrian Alps, but without the element of combat.

EASTERN EUROPE AND THE BALKANS

Lively festivals, involving parades of hideously masked characters blowing on horns, are encountered in Hungary. In Fejér, for example, cloth masks with straggling beards and eyebrows are worn under battered felt hats decorated with ribbons. Carved and painted female masks, which have much in common with those of neighbouring Austria, are also worn.

The tradition of holding noisy mid-winter festivals continues in Romania, especially in the northern county of Maramureş. Shaggy devil headdresses with horns are worn by the participants, as well as disguises incorporating other features such as Second World War gas masks. Masks representing 'old men' are known on both the Transylvanian and Moldavian sides of the Carpathian mountains. Made of hessian, these masks are furnished with seed teeth and hemp fibre beards. The Romanian hobby-horse, *caluşar*, which is associated with All Souls' Night, also performs during the mid-winter festivals. Characters representing a fool and a 'man-woman' accompany the hobby-horse, as does a troupe of dancers who

engage in a ritual battle.

Turon, another festival which includes a hobby-horse, is observed by Polish peasants. It takes place in the period following Christmas and is thought to have its origins in the veneration of the Slavic winter god, Radegast. The festival is named after *Turon*, a fabulous creature from Polish mythology. *Turon*'s head is usually carved from a single block of wood, to which a hinged jaw is attached. The head may be painted with bright colours and the ears are sometimes studded with nails. As is the case with other hobby-horses, the mask is supported on a pole and the carrier is shrouded with a cloth. *Turon* is the most popular of the animal disguises assumed by the revellers as they go from house to house singing carols and receiving refreshments. Other masks worn by villagers include representations of bears, wolves and goats.

In common with other Slavic peoples, the Bulgarians make masks resembling animals such as bears, foxes, wolves, birds and other fantastic creatures. These masks are worn during New Year festivities, especially in the west of the country. Of particular significance in Bulgaria are the agrarian rituals, which are thought to have roots in ancient Thrace. Held on the first Sunday before Lent (that is, at the beginning of the new agricultural year), these celebrations involve large groups of

Hungary, gourd, early twentieth century
Parades of devils are traditionally held in rural regions of Hungary. This painted mask (**left**) was probably made for a child.

Romania, dried calabash
Inexpensive materials are often used to make masks in rural areas. This mask (**above**) has large teeth made from beans. The expression is both comic and sinister and the mask has much in common with clown-devil masks from other areas of Europe.

Northern Transylvania, Romania, wool, cloth, beans
This pair of typical Maramureș masks (**right**) represent grotesque devils. The masks are thought to frighten away the evil spirits of winter.

Switzerland, painted wood, c. 1900
*Masks representing animals are worn in the high Alpine regions of Switzerland. This pig mask (**above**) comes from the mountainous canton of Graubündan.*

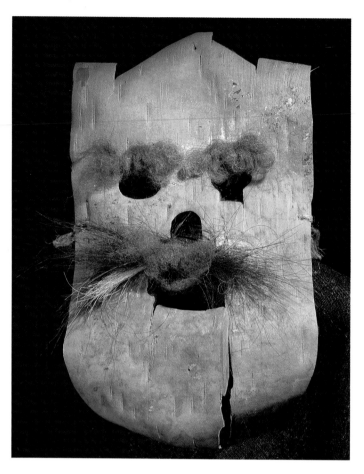

Sweden, painted wood, fibre
*Although European masqueraders often perform plays that have Christian elements, the masking tradition dates back to pagan festivals. This mask (**left**) represents Judas Iscariot.*

Bern, Switzerland, c. 1960
*This large mask (**right**) belongs to the comic European masquerade tradition. It has a helmet which is too small, and a foolish grin. In mock-heroic fashion, a knife is held between the oversized teeth.*

men dressed as both domestic and wild animals. During the festival the men jump, so that the wheat will grow tall and make a great deal of noise, to scare away the old year and its evil forces. Many of the cloth masks have moustaches and beards made from scraps of fur, feathers and hemp fibres. They may also be embellished with swirling lines of small metal discs. Some of the performers, wearing horned sheepskin masks representing oxen, are harnessed to wooden ploughs.

The Greeks traditionally mark the beginning of the new agricultural year with rituals that resemble those of Bulgaria and other Balkan neighbours. A *kalogheroi* dancer of Thrace, for example, wears a bonnet made of fox or wolf fur. Goatskins, equipped with eyeholes, are hung from the headgear, covering the performer's shoulders and chest. Numerous bells are slung from the waist and in Skyros phallic-shaped rods are carried. Masquerades are also found in the northern provinces, where masks are worn representing characters such as the devil, the Vlach (Romanian shepherd), the Moor and the female doctor.

ITALY AND SPAIN

A wide variety of masquerades are known in Italy, including many that are associated with rural rites. An interesting example of the latter, which symbolizes dying vegetation, is traditionally performed in Perugia. It involves an 'old woman' wearing a tree-bark mask, who encounters some wood-cutters. Mistaking the 'old woman' for an oak tree, the wood-

cutters proceed to cut her up, despite the intervention of various other characters. The mistake is eventually realized and several attempts are made to revive the woman, but without success, and finally the doctor is called in. He wears a wooden mask and wooden shoes and has a false tail.

Although Italy's rural masquerades are fascinating, what the country is best known for, in terms of masks, is the *Commedia dell' arte*, a theatrical genre that flourished from the sixteenth century to the eighteenth century. Its constellation of characters, many of whom wore masks, remained the same, whatever the changes in the plot. Harlequin, who is thought to be related to the clown-devils of traditional masquerades, usually wore a demoniacal half-mask made of leather or waxed cardboard. He can be distinguished by his bushy eyebrows and moustache, snub nose and the large carbuncle on his forehead. Brighella, the cunning servant, wore an animal-like mask with slit eyes and a crooked nose. Pulcinella, the buffoon, wore a bony mask with a hooked nose and prominent eyebrows. The doctor, who wore academic dress, usually had a half mask with a bulbous nose and flaccid cheeks.

In addition to the *Commedia dell' arte*, Italy is also well known for the Venetian carnival of the seventeenth and eighteenth centuries. The carnival began just after Christmas and finished towards the end of June, and during this period black or white masks could be worn by both rich and poor alike. The wearers of masks were entitled to certain privileges, such

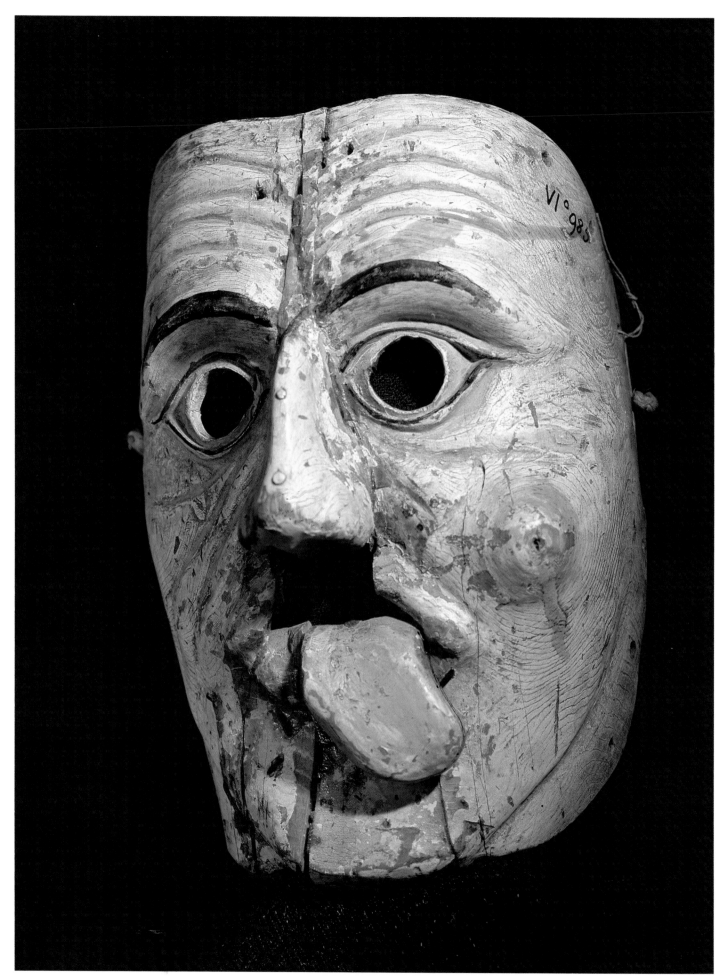

Italy, painted wood, mid-twentieth century
*This grotesque mask (**left**) has a large lolling tongue and an unsightly carbuncle on one cheek. The masks of the famous* Commedia dell'Arte *had their origins in traditional masks like this one.*

Sardinia, Italy, carved wood
*This folk festival mask (**right**), which may represent a character from the spirit world, has been blackened with smoke.*

as the right to engage in gambling from eight- or nine-o-clock in the morning, providing their faces remained covered.

Like the Italians, the Spaniards have a distinguished tradition in masking, especially during religious festivals. In Holy Week, for example, penitents wear tall pointed hoods equipped with eyeholes. Made in silk, these hoods mask the face and cover the shoulders. Each religious fraternity has its place in the Holy Week processions, and members of the different brotherhoods can be distinguished by their badges and the colour of their hoods.

The Spanish also wear masks to perform the *Morisca* (Moorish dance), an important masquerade that has been known on the Iberian peninsula for at least 400 years. It represents the battle between the Moors and the Christians and is enacted during Catholic festivals, notably at carnival time, during San Juan's Day and Corpus Christi. A variety of painted faces are worn, though some performers use make-up or hide their faces with bandannas.

What is interesting about the *Morisca*, in a wider European context, is the way in which Spanish elements appear to have been borrowed by other European peoples and adapted to local circumstances. The *Morisca* is closely related to other masquerades, especially those involving stick or sword dances, such as the Portuguese *Mouriscada* and the Basque *Mascarades*. Many other European masquerade traditions are also thought to have their roots in Spain.

BUYER'S GUIDE

Masks as a category in the collecting field are very different from such categories as dolls or cameras, in that there are no dealers (to my knowledge) who specialize in masks alone and it is not as yet a subject to which auction houses devote sales exclusively (although this may occur if they are called upon to disperse a particular collection). The main auction houses in Europe have sales devoted to tribal art covering the arts of Africa, the Americas, the Pacific, Indonesia and parts of mainland Asia and these will invariably include several masks. In New York similar sales are held, with separate sales often devoted to North American Indian art. A Japanese mask might appear in a sale devoted to Japanese or Oriental art, a Sri Lankan mask in a sale of Indian or Oriental art and so on.

One of the best ways to find out about the forthcoming sales at an auction house is to subscribe to the catalogues, although this could be an expensive exercise. Japanese masks, for instance, do not appear very frequently at auction and to buy and scan the pages of all the Japanese catalogues would be a waste of time and money. A more sensible alternative is to notify the auction house of your interests and ask them to let you know when an example of a particular type of mask you are interested in is coming up for sale.

It is also a good idea to find a dealer you can trust, although these also tend to specialize in specific areas such as African or Oriental art. Through a network of contacts, however, they may well be able to help with masks from areas outside their sphere.

Before starting a collection the novice must decide on the scope he wishes his collection to cover. This will be dictated by the availability of the various types of mask on the market and, of course, on the collector's budget. Masks from Africa are relatively numerous and it would be possible to form a collection covering a wide geographical area without spending more than £100 (US $165) on any one example, although of course the quality would not be particularly good. Prices for African masks run upwards not only to four- or five- but even to six-figure sums. Sri Lankan masks are relatively undervalued at auction and some very fine and old specimens occasionally appear on the market, often for no more than £200–£300 (US$330–$495). North American Indian masks are less affordable for the collector with a modest budget. The number of collectors in North America and the relatively small number of masks that appear on the market means that prices are usually in excess of £1000 (US $1650).

Punu, Gabon, wood
*This dance mask (**above**) from the Ogowe River region is less oriental in appearance than most examples.*
Height: 9½in (24cm)

Sri Lanka, wood
*This fine mask (**right**) may represent Garuda, the mythical bird of Indian legend. Its size suggests that it was paraded, rather than worn, at ceremonies.*
Height: 54½in (138.5cm)
Sotheby's London 1983, £1000

Sepik River, Papua New Guinea, wood
*This carved, mask-like piece (**above**) would have been worn as a charm.*
Height: 2¾in (7cm)

For the new collector it would be wise to familiarize himself with as many examples of a particular type of mask as possible before actually buying. There are many excellent books and exhibition catalogues to refer to, some of which are very specific in scope and in the recent past their number has increased dramatically. Of course, it would be dangerous to base your judgement on what you have seen in a book or catalogue alone. Visiting museum collections is also helpful and here you will have the opportunity of seeing types of masks even the collector with unlimited funds is unlikely ever to have the opportunity of owning. Often the museum will quote collection data very useful for comparative purposes. The new collector will thus be able to learn to recognize features and signs

that indicate the age of a particular mask, information often absent when a mask is offered for sale.

Many small provincial museums have particularly fine collections of masks that have come to them through a local benefactor, and it is often a great surprise to come across them in unlikely places. However, bear in mind that the curators of such museums often have responsibility for a far greater variety of materials than the auction-house expert or dealer and there is consequently just as much scope for errors in identification and attribution as there is in the commercial world.

Visiting museums is all very well, but seeing a mask behind glass is a poor substitute for being able to handle it. Therefore, previewing and attending a

*Dan, Ivory Coast, wood, fibre (**left**) Height: 5in (12.5cm)*

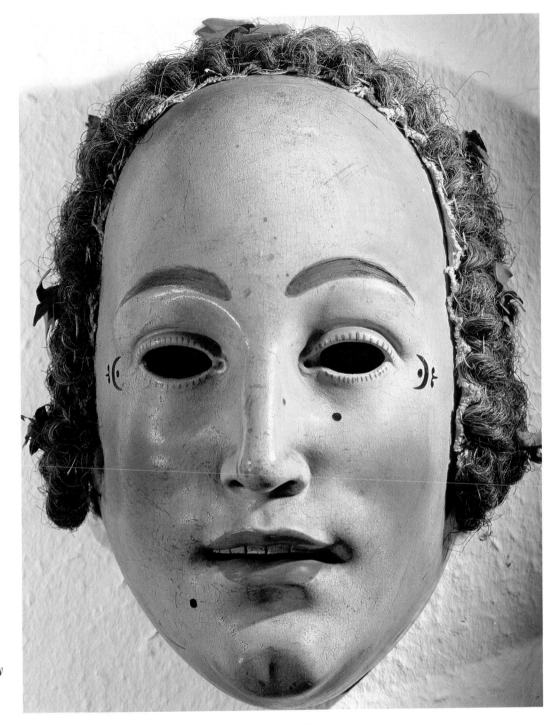

Black Forest, Germany, carved and painted wood, early nineteenth century Masks representing beautiful people are also traditionally worn in the rowdy midwinter Schemenlaufen *festivals. This high-quality mask (**right**) is attributed to Dominikus Ackerman.*

public auction provide an invaluable opportunity for the collector to 'get the feel' of a good mask. In a relatively small field such as tribal art, auctions are also something of a social event, providing a good opportunity to meet dealers and collectors both from home and abroad. It is always interesting to hear other people's views on a particular piece, but if you are eavesdropping in the hope of learning something to your advantage, treat such opinions with caution: people often play their cards close to their chests at auction and it is common to hear someone speak scathingly about a piece at a preview only to see them bidding for it at the sale, or similarly to wax lyrical about a mask and then fail to raise their hand even when it appears to be selling cheaply (after all, it

might be theirs!).

As a rule sales are held on week days, which is an inconvenience for many private collectors. Increasingly, however, auction houses are providing an opportunity for viewing in the evenings or at weekends in order to encourage more private buyers. If you cannot attend a sale personally it is possible to leave a bid with the auction house, although it is very difficult to decide the price you are prepared to pay a day or two before the sale. Collectors often ask how much they should leave on a particular lot. It is a good idea to imagine yourself telephoning after the sale to find out the results. If you leave a bid for a certain amount and then find out that the mask was sold for a higher price that you would still have been

prepared to pay, then you should have left at least that much. This may sound obvious, but it is extraordinary how many people leave a bid to cover a lot in case it sells cheaply and then are disappointed when it goes for more than they left but less than they really feel it was worth to them.

Of course, it is much more exciting to attend the sale yourself and, contrary to popular belief, there is really little danger of an auctioneer interpreting a scratch of the nose as a bid. Should you make an error, however, and you find you have bought the wrong lot, make it known to the auctioneer straight away and do not wait until after the sale when it is too late to be remedied.

Most auction catalogues now include estimated prices for each lot. The buyer must bear in mind that these are only a guide and are perhaps the opinion of only one individual. Various factors play a part in arriving at these estimates. If an owner simply wants to get rid of a single lot or of a collection and wants to avoid the risk of a lot being unsold, the estimates may be conservative to encourage bidding. On the other hand, an owner may consign a particular lot for sale with a price in mind that may be a little optimistic. So it would be wrong to think you should pay no more than the top estimate or that it would necessarily be worth buying a lot because it is selling below the estimate. Experts make mistakes, too, and one of the excitements at a sale is to see a 'sleeper' with a modest estimate suddenly take off, leaving the audience gasping and the expert looking a little embarrassed. This may in any case not be entirely the fault of the auction house. It only takes two determined bidders to push the price far beyond what most buyers might consider reasonable.

Before you decide what, if anything, you wish to bid for, ask the expert in charge of the sale what his or her opinion is as to the value of a lot (and preferably consult any other person whose judgement you have come to trust). By the time of the preview the expert may be able to give you a more up-to-date estimate based on people's reactions at the time and, if you know beforehand that the lot in which you are most interested is going to be way beyond your reach, you may prefer to concentrate on another. Decide before the sale what you are going to bid for and how much you are prepared to pay for it—and then stick to your decision. With perhaps up to 400 lots to get through in a single session the auctioneer has to keep up a fairly rapid pace and if you have not decided an upper limit on a particular lot it is easy to find yourself paying considerably more than you intended to. Bear in mind also that you will have to pay the auctioneer's commission on the hammer price and possibly a sales tax.

It would be nice to think that, having bought your mask, you can then expect it to appreciate in value to keep pace with inflation. I have often been asked the likes of 'If I buy this mask and bring it back in five years time how much do you think it will fetch?' My answer to such questions has always been that if that is your concern you would be better off keeping your money in a bank. Buy your mask because it gives you pleasure to own it; the purchase of your mask should not be disappointing if the market collapsed in a year or two. It is very difficult to predict which categories are on the increase and which are likely to drop in popularity. In recent years masks have followed the trend of other fields: the very best command very high prices that often outpace inflation, while more pedestrian examples from Africa, of which there is a steady supply, have fared less well, their prices often remaining fairly static.

One of the factors in assessing the value of a mask is its provenance, and in recent years this has become increasingly important, due no doubt to the increasing competence of fakers. Many buyers are reassured by a good early provenance, which reduces the onerous task of having to rely on one's own judgement. If it is known where a mask was collected, when and by whom it can affect the price considerably. A valuable provenance does not simply mean that the name of the person who collected the mask in the field is known. It may simply have belonged to a particular collector or even have passed through the hands of a well-known dealer. Masks that had once belonged to the artist, Maurice de Vlaminck, have recently been sold at auction in Paris for sums far in excess of their intrinsic value. Similarly, masks that have passed through the hands of the English dealers, Webster and Oldman, at the beginning of this century might today fetch two or three times the sums of similar masks without this significant connection.

A word of warning is needed here, however. You should take care when confronted with old labels, since it is not unknown for unscrupulous dealers to remove old collection labels from items of relatively small value and affix them to more valuable objects. This has happened in the case of items from the Beasley Collection. Fortunately, Beasley kept ledgers in which he recorded against his inventory number such information as an item's description and where and when he purchased it. The ledgers are now in the British Museum and it is possible to check the label against his entry. Of course, exactly what constitutes an early provenance will depend on the area from which the mask comes. The vast majority of African, south-east Asian or Pacific masks seen on the market or even in museum collections will have been collect-

Bavaria, Germany, carved and painted wood, early twentieth century
*The noise of jangling bells, according to tradition, is thought to frighten away the evil spirits of winter. This mask (**left**) was worn during* Schemenlaufen *festivals.*

Alpine, painted wood
The midwinter festivals
that are held in the Alps to
frighten off the
accumulated spirits of
winter are usually noisy.
This mask has a hole in the
mouth so that the wearer
could blow on a pipe.

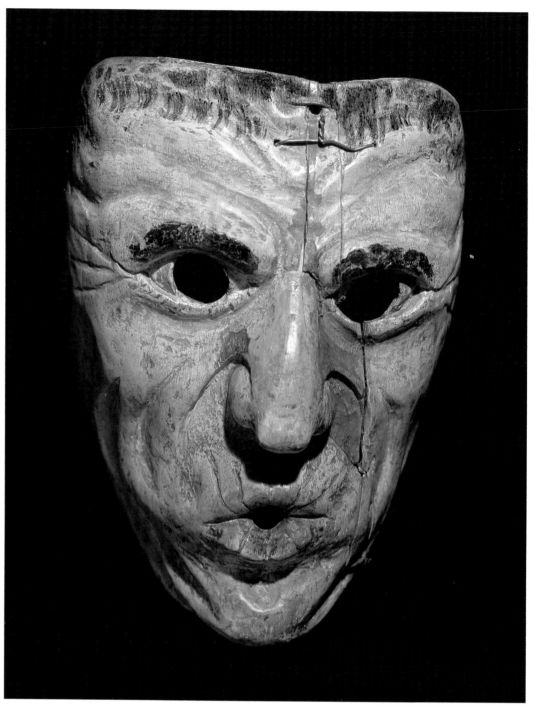

ed this century and an early twentieth-century provenance therefore should not be considered too late to be of significance but can make a considerable difference to the price. The use of masks for traditional purposes declined in many cultures after European contact and was revived only in relatively recent times, sometimes due to a renewed pride in a people's cultural heritage (though often commercial considerations have played a part).

It was in the 1950's and 1960s that production of many types of African masks for the art market was at its height and consequently a pre-1940 date should not be regarded as too late to be of significance. On the island of Pentecost in Vanuatu, the carving of masks has been revived only in the past twenty years,

while some fairly good fakes may have originated in Europe even more recently. Consequently you would not have to trace the history of a mask back too far to be reasonably sure it was an old example.

Unfortunately, there are a great many fake masks on the market from many continents. 'Fake' is a term to be used with caution. A 'fake' is something intended to deceive and is not synonymous with 'modern'. It must be remembered that many of the masking traditions of Africa, Europe and Central and South America are still thriving today.

There are no hard and fast rules to guide the novice collector in spotting a fake. You can learn to recognize certain signs from experience in handling masks, but even experienced collectors and dealers will often

Alpine, carved and painted wood, cloth, early twentieth century
This mask represents a poor, old woman. According to popular tradition, Alpine mask makers sometimes designed caricatures based on real people.

disagree over authenticity. The most telling signs of the authenticity of a mask are not on the front but on the back, a view one is denied in the museum, and the collector should take full use here of the opportunity to handle tribal art presented at auction previews. It may be a little dangerous to generalize, but as a rule there is no need for the carver of a mask to pay much attention to the reverse; this will not be seen by the spectator in the masquerade or play and, as very little of the surface of the mask comes into contact with the face of the wearer, there is no need to smooth the surface for comfort. Consequently, in many good old masks the adzing is clearly visible on the reverse, whether neatly or roughly executed. Fake masks are often given an overall smoothing of the back and also

of the edges to give the impression of having been worn over a long period of time. On a genuine old mask, however, the wear will not be uniform over the whole surface, and the lower edges that might come in contact with the face may appear darker and glossier than the rest of the back surface. It should be remembered, however, that a mask may have been collected before it had had much use, so signs of wear are by no means an essential requirement for an old or genuine mask. In the case of many fakes from Zaire the back is also scorched or blackened with soot. It is a good idea to smell the surface. Does it smell as though it has really been in an old colonial family for generations or does it smell as though it came out of Africa last week?

91

CARE AND MAINTENANCE

Damage is perhaps less important when buying masks than other objects. Tropical climates are unsuitable for the conservation of the soft, light woods usually employed by carvers in parts of Africa and a certain amount of damage is almost inevitable. Termite damage is also common and is positively encouraged by carvers of fakes in West Africa as a sign of 'authenticity'. Light woods are also attractive to other insects and masks should be checked for signs of activity. Two years ago I set up a shield from the highlands of New Guinea in our photographic studio to be photographed and was surprised to see a fat bug crawling out from the wood, presumably brought to life by the heat from the spotlights. The woods are also prone to damage by woodworm and any evidence of infestation should be checked to ensure it is not live. Damage sustained during a masquerade can positively add to the value of a mask where a neat mend by a native craftsman is evident.

Restoration should always be left to a professional and should only be undertaken if the damage is so severe as to detract considerably from the mask's appearance. Evidence of restoration will make many collectors suspicious and therefore may not add to the resale value of a mask. The cost may also be prohibitive and it will often be difficult, if not impossible, to match exactly the materials used. Always photograph the mask, preferably from more than one angle, before any restoration is undertaken.

Many of the masks described in this book were made for use in a single performance and durability ws therefore not a consideration of the carver. Many masks are very fragile and, in many cases, even cleaning with a duster may not be possible. A solid wood surface can be dusted but not if the mask has a crusty patina, which may flake. Great care should be taken if the mask is painted; many types of paints such as those used on the north-west coast of America are not as permanent as modern synthetic paints. If the mask has an old label attached, giving details of its provenance or of a collection through which it has passed, take great care of it since to lose it would reduce the mask's value. Bronze masks should not be cleaned with metal polish, as removal of the original patination will reduce their value; this fate has befallen many of the bronze hip masks brought back to England from Benin at the end of the last century.

Masks of bark cloth or fibre, such as those from South America or parts of New Guinea, are often too delicate for any sort of cleaning by anyone other than a professional. A reputable dealer, auction house or museum may be able to suggest a specialist to tackle the job, though it is likely to be costly. If you are going away for any length of time and such a mask is on display uncovered, it is worthwhile to cover it loosely with a thin sheet of plastic to reduce the accumulation of dust but to allow the circulation of air as, should moisture be trapped inside, this will cause damage. Avoid storing or displaying masks where they will be subject to fluctuations in temperature or humidity, since this is likely to cause splits in wooden masks and will cause natural fibres to become brittle and eventually decompose. The application of a layer of varnish to some wooden masks brought back to Europe earlier this century was not uncommon and can be removed by a professional restorer without harm to the original patina underneath.

CATALOGUING AND DISPLAY

Although masks may not be as obvious a target for a thief as silver or jewellery, they have nevertheless been stolen in the past from museums, private collectors and auction houses. Without a photographic record of your collection it is very difficult to describe a mask sufficiently well, either in writing or verbally, to enable it to be identified. I face a similar problem every week with people trying to describe a mask or figure over the telephone in the hope that I will be able to visualize it and give them some idea of its value. Take photographs of every mask in your collection, preferably from more than one angle, so that these can be circulated to auction houses and dealers in the event that they are stolen. Keep the photographs together with a record of when and where you bought the mask, how much you paid for it and any other information you may have concerning its history, such as when and where it was collected and by whom. Since today this type of data can often affect an object's price, an auction house or dealer will usually try to obtain this information when they first obtain the mask (but if they have not, ask them if they can supply any more information beyond what they have already quoted). If the mask came from a private source it may be possible to make contact with the previous owner. Although auction houses will not release the names of vendors they will often have no objection to forwarding a letter to a vendor on your behalf and will probably be able to tell you whether or not this effort is worthwhile.

Not all masks can be categorized definitely as belonging to one particular tribal group. For many geographical areas much work is still to be done by scholars. Some masks may in fact combine features of various tribal styles. It is therefore worthwhile keeping a record of any similar masks you come across in museums or published in books or catalogues.

The obvious way to display a mask is simply to hang it on the wall. The wall would have to be of a uniform colour if the mask is to be clearly visible and it should not be prone to damp or condensation. It would also be unwise to hang a mask above a radiator, where the constant change in temperature is likely to cause damage. A small and delicate mask may look lost on a vast expanse of wall and it could not be seen to its best advantage in such a position. Many masks are not designed to be worn on the front of the face in a vertical position and these would therefore also be unsuitable for a wall display. A Yoruba *gelede* mask, for example, would be facing towards the floor if hung on a wall, and would be seen to much better advantage if simply lain on a shelf.

Many buyers of masks prefer to mount masks on stands rather than hang them on the wall; this is particularly suitable for small masks, which can then be rotated and seen from all angles. Most stands consist of a simple metal loop that curves around inside the border of the mask with the ends slotting into holes found in the borders of most masks. This loop is joined to a vertical support inserted into a rectangular or wooden block. Dealers and auction houses have frequent cause to use the services of a stand maker and should be able to recommend one to you. Many are very skilled and Inagaki, a Japanese stand maker who died shortly after the Second World War and who specialized in stands for works of tribal art, is now so highly regarded that his stands can add considerably to the price of a work of art.

MUSEUMS

Many museums in Europe and North America, both small and large, have fine collections of masks, some broad in scope and others quite limited, often reflecting the colonial past of the countries in which they are to be found. Just a sample is listed here.

UNITED KINGDOM

Museum of Mankind, London
Horniman Museum, London
Pitt Rivers Museum, Oxford
Cambridge University Museum of Archaeology and Anthropology, Cambridge
Liverpool Museum, Liverpool
Hunterian Museum, Glasgow
Royal Museum of Scotland, Edinburgh
Brighton Art Gallery and Museum, Brighton
Ipswich Museum, Ipswich
Manchester Museum, Manchester
Powell-Cotton Museum, Birchington
Royal Albert Memorial Museum and Art Gallery, Exeter
Ulster Museum, Belfast

NORTH AMERICA

American Museum of Natural History, New York
Brooklyn Museum, New York
Metropolitan Museum of Art, New York
Buffalo Museum of Science, New York
Cleveland Museum of Art, Cleveland
Dallas Museum of Fine Arts, Dallas
Detroit Institute of Arts, Detroit
The Denver Art Museum, Denver
Field Museum of Natural History, Chicago
Indiana University Art Museum, Bloomington
Museum of Cultural History, Los Angeles
Seattle Art Museum, Seattle
Peabody Museum of Archaeology and Ethnology, Cambridge
Lowie Museum of Anthropology, Berkeley
National Museum of African Art, Washington D.C.
Royal Ontario Museum, Toronto

EUROPE

Musée de l'Homme, Paris
Musée National des Arts africains at océaniens, Paris
Musée Royal de l'Afrique Centrale, Tervuren, Belgium
Rautenstrauch-Joest-Museum für Völkerkunde, Cologne
Museum für Völkerkunde, Berlin
Museum für Völkerkunde, Frankfurt
Staatliches Museum für Völkerkunde, Munich
Linden Museum für Lander und Völkerkunde, Stuttgart
Museum für Völkerkunde, Freiburg im Breisgau
Hamburgisches Museum für Völkerkunde, Hamburg
Museum Rietberg, Zurich
Museum für Völkerkunde, Basel
Museum für Völkerkunde, Vienna
Rijksmuseum voor Volkenkunde, Leiden
Koninklijk Instituut voor den Tropen Museum, Amsterdam
Museum voor Volkenkunde, Rotterdam
Volkenkundig Museum Nusantara, Delft
Museo Nazionale Preistorico Etnografico "L. Pigorini", Rome
Museo Nazionale di Antropologia e di Etnologia, Florence
National Museum of Denmark, Copenhagen
Museu de Etnologia, Lisbon
National Museum of Ireland, Dublin
Musée International du Carnaval et due Masque, Binche

BIBLIOGRAPHY

Ali, A.K., The Hidden Power of Shaman Masks from Sarawak, *Connaissance des Arts Tribaux* no.19, Geneva

Barbier, J.P. and Newton, D. (editors), *Islands and Ancestors*, New York, 1988

Bastin, M–L., *La Sculpture Tschokwe*, Meudon, 1982

Biebuyck, D., *Lega Culture*, Los Angeles, 1973

Bleakley, R., *African Masks*, London, 1978

Bourgeois, A.P., *Art of the Yaka and Suku*, Meudon, 1984

Cameron, E.L., Sala Mpasu Masks, *African Arts* Vol. XXII no.1, Los Angeles, 1988

Cole, H.M. and Aniakor, C.C., *Ibo Arts Community and Cosmos*, Los Angeles, 1984

Cole, H.M., *I am not myself: the Art of African Masquerade*, Los Angeles, 1985

Cornet, J., *Art Royal Kuba*, Milan, 1982

Cordry, D.B., *Mexican Masks*, Austin, 1980

Dark, P.J., *Kilenge, Life and Art*, London, 1974

Deacon, A.B., *Malekula, A Vanishing Peoples in The New Hebrides*, London, 1934

Dockstader, F.J., *South American Indian Art*, London, 1967

Donne, J.B., Ceylon Masks in the British Museum, *The Connoisseur*, April, 1978

Eckholm, G.F., *Ancient Mexico and Central America*, New York, 1970

Ezra, K., *Art of the Dogon*, New York, 1988

Fagg, W.B., *Tribes and Forms in African Art*, Paris, 1965

Fagg, W.B., *Masques d'Afrique dans les collections du Musée Barbier-Müller*, Geneva, 1980

Fagg, W.B., Pemberton, J., and Holcombe, B., *Yoruba Sculpture of West Africa*, New York, 1982

Fischer, E. and Himmelheber, H., *The Arts of the Dan in West Africa*, Zurich, 1984

Goonatilleka, M.H., *Masks and Mask Systems of Sri Lanka*, Colombo, 1978

Guiart, J., *Arts of the South Pacific*, London, 1963

Hasibuan, J., *Art et Culture Batak*, Jakarta, 1985

Hersak, D., *Songye Masks and Figure Sculpture*, London, 1985

Heurley, E., *Pearls and Savages*, New York, 1924

Himmelheber, H., *Art et Artists Batshiok*, Brousse, 1939

Holm, Bill, *Spirits and Ancestors*, Seattle, 1987

Holy, L., *Masks and Figures from Eastern and Southern Africa*, London, 1967

Kecskési, M., *African Masterpieces and Selected Works from Munich: The Staatliches Museum für Völkerkunde*, New York, 1987

King, J.C.H., *Portrait Masks from the Northwest Coast of America*, London, 1979

Lamp, F., The Art of the Baga: A Preliminary Enquiry, *African Arts*, Vol. XIX, no.2, Los Angeles, 1986

Levi-Strauss, C,. *The Way of the Masks*, London, 1983

Lewis, P., The Social Context of Art in Northern New Ireland, *Fieldiana: Anthropology*, Vol. 58, Chicago, 1969

Lucas, H., *Ceylon Masken*, Kassel, 1958

Lucas, H., *Lamaïstische Masken*, Kassel, 1962

Mead, S.M., ed., *Exploring the Visual Art of Oceania*, Honolulu, 1979

Moore, D.R., *The Torres Straits Collection of A.C. Haddon*, London, 1984

Newton, D., *Crocodile and Cassowary*, New York, 1971

Northern, T., *The Art of the Cameroon*, Washington, 1984

Pannier, F. and Mangin, S., *Masques de l'Himalaya du Primitif au Classique*, 1989

Perrois, L., *La Statuaire Fan*, Paris, 1972

Perrois, L., *Ancestral Art of Gabon from the Collections of the Barbier-Müller Museum*, Geneva, 1985

Phelps, S.J., *Art and Artefacts of the Pacific, Africa and the Americas, The James Hooper Collection*, London, 1976

Redinha, J., *Campanha Etnografica ao Tchiboco*, Lisbon, 1953/5

Roy, C., *Art of the Upper Volta Rivers*, Meudon, 1987

Schmalenbach, W. (editor), *African Art: The Barbier-Müller Collection*, Geneva, 1988

Schmitz, C.A., *Oceanic Art*, New York, 1971

Stöhr, W., *Art of the Archaic Indonesians*, Geneva, 1982

Timmermans, P., *Les Lwalwa*, Tervuren, 1967

Vogel, S. (editor), *For Spirits and Kings, African Art from the Paul and Ruth Tishman Collection*, New York, 1981

Wardwels, A., *The Art of the Sepik River*, Chicago, 1971

INDEX

ACKNOWLEDGEMENTS

The author and publishers would like to thank the private individuals, museums and other establishments for granting permission to reproduce photographs in this book on the following pages:

6 – American Museum of Natural History; 7 – P A Ferrazzini/Musee Barbier-Müller; 8 – Studio Lemaire/ van Bussel Archive; 9 – (left) van Bussel Archive, (right) van Bussel Archive; 10 – Private Collection; 11 – van Bussel Archive; 12 – Private Collection; 13 – Christie's London; 15–(left) British Museum, (right) Christie's London; 16 – British Museum; 17 – British Museum; 18 – British Museum; 19 – British Museum; 20 – Sotheby's London; 21 – (left) Christie's London, (right) Christie's London; 22 – Archive Leloup; 23 – (left) Christie's London, (right) Private Collection; 24 – Christie's London; 25 – Christie's London; 26 – A C Cooper Ltd; 27 – (left) Christie's London, (right) courtesy Entwistle, London; 28 – Christie's London; 29 – (left) Museum Rietberg, Zurich, (right) Christie's New York; 30 – (above) Asselberghs/Musee Barbier-Müller, (below) P A Ferrazzini/Musee Barbier-Müller; 31 – (left) Sotheby's London, (right) Christie's New York; 32 – (above) courtesy Entwistle, London, (below) Christie's London; 33 – Christie's London; 34 – (left) Christopher Taylor, (right) Christie's London; 36 – Christie's London; 37 – van Bussel Archive; 38 – courtesy Entwistle, London; 39 – courtesy Entwistle/Photo Werner Forman, London; 40 – (left) Christie's London, (right) Christie's London; 41 – Christie's New York; 42 – Christie's London; 43 – Seattle Art Museum/Katherine White Collection; 44 – Peter Adler; 45 – Studio Lemaire/van Bussel Archive; 46 – (above) Christie's London, (below) Peter Adler; 47 – (above) Christie's London, (below) van Bussel Collection; 48-9 – British Museum; 49 – Studio Lemaire/van Bussel Archive; 52 – van Bussel Collection; 53 – van Bussel Collection; 54 – University of East Anglia/ Sainsbury Centre; 55 – (left) Sotheby's London, (above right) Studio Lemaire/van Bussel Collection, (below right) University of East Anglia/Sainsbury Centre: 56 – British Museum; 57 – British Museum; 58 – A C Cooper Ltd; 59 – van Bussel Collection; 60 – British Museum; 63 – (left) Christie's London, (right) Christie's London; 64 – Christie's London; 65 – Christie's London; 66-7 – American Museum of Natural History; 67 – (above) Christie's London, (below) Christie's London; 69 – (left) American Museum of Natural History, (above right) Private Collection, (below right) British Museum; 70 – (left) British Museum, (right) British Museum; 71 – Museum für Völkerkunde, Berlin; 72 – British Museum; 73 – (left) British Museum, (above right) Christie's London, (below right) Christie's London; 74-83 inclusive – Claus Hansmann Archive; 84 – van Bussel Archive; 85 – Sotheby's London; 87 – Claus Hansmann Archive; 88 – Claus Hansmann Archive; 90 – Claus Hansmann Archive; 91 – Claus Hansmann Archive.